THE GREAT HERESY

ARTHUR GUIRDHAM

The Great Heresy

Index compiled by Lyn Greenwood

SAFFRON WALDEN
THE C.W. DANIEL COMPANY LIMITED

First published in 1977 by Neville Spearman (Jersey) Limited

This edition published by
The C.W. Daniel Company Limited
1 Church Path, Saffron Walden, Essex, CB10 1JP, England in 1993

ISBN 0 85207 271 6

Printed in England by
Hillman Printers Ltd., Frome, Somerset

CONTENTS

Part One

Part Two

PART ONE

CHAPTER ONE

If one asks the average Englishman why the Inquisition was founded he invariably answers to combat the beginnings of Protestantism. As like as not he will prefix the noun by the adjective Spanish and recall desperately the lot of English sailors and merchants who fell into the hands of the Holy Office in the sixteenth century. The Inquisition predates the Elizabethan age by more than three centuries. It was born long before the world had heard the names Lollard or Hussite, let alone Lutheran, Calvinist or Protestant. It was founded by St. Dominic as near as we can estimate in 1233. There had previously been a form of Inquisition presided over by Catholic bishops but this never revealed the efficiency and ruthlessness subsequently attained when the Holy Office was recruited from the Dominican order.

The Inquisition was directed against the Cathars, a sect little known in this country until recent years and more commonly referred to as the Albigenses. Formerly, to those who had heard the name, Catharism was a heresy of limited scope which was ruthlessly extirpated by the Catholic Church. The situation was confusing for the student because the word Cathar suggested to some a dour and self-mutilating asceticism while to others the name was associated with a vague aura of scandal. Up to a decade ago few realised that Catharism was a coherent and cultivated religious philosophy which, in the regions in which it was established, threatened the very existence of the Roman Church.

This is in no sense one of those 'if only' books which suggest that, had circumstances been propitious, this or that obscure religious or political creed would have swept the world instead of wilting unnoticed by the wayside. Catharism was already predominant in the Languedoc of the thirteenth century and in the other possessions and dependencies of the Counts of

3

Toulouse who at this time presided over the richest, most cultivated and most sophisticated civilisation in Europe. It must be remembered that Toulouse, in the beginning of the thirteenth century, was far wealthier and more populated than Paris or London or than any other city than Rome. In the domains of other mediaeval lords Catharism was tolerated and encouraged. It was particularly strong in the area presided over by the Trencavel family which included the highly populated cities of Carcassonne and Béziers. It was also well established in the neighbourhood of Albi and Agen. While pockets of Catharism were scattered all over what is now called France it was mainly concentrated between the Dordogne and the Pyrenees on a north–south axis. Its influence was paramount from Agen in the west to Béziers in the east, and very strong in the Massif Central and in what is now known as Provence.

It is probable that Catharism was as well established in north Italy as in southern France. By the beginning of the thirteenth century it had taken root in the big towns, such as Milan, Turin and Florence, where many members of the city councils were either practitioners of or well disposed to the heresy. There were numerous other centres of Catharism in northern Italy. The heresy was indeed disseminated throughout the peninsula and reached as far south as Sicily. Unfortunately we have less knowledge of Catharism in Italy than in France. Less has been written on the subject in Italy and access to sources of reference seems altogether more difficult. I have heard it said by French workers in this field that the Vatican still holds depositions related to Catharism but is reluctant to permit access to them. Set against this is the fact that we owe the discovery in Italy of one of the basic items of Cathar literature to the efforts of a diligent Dominican, Father Dondaine.* In this book I am mostly concerned with Catharism in the Languedoc which was its heart and soul and where its roots were most resistant. It must be understood that the Languedoc of the Middle Ages represented a far richer, more powerful and geographically greater entity than the region described by the same name in the twentieth century.

* Le Rituel de Florence.

4

We are not indebted to Cathar sources for our knowledge that Catharism was so widely and deeply established in the Midi of France and in northern Italy. Cathar records and literature were as ruthlessly destroyed by the Church as were the living exponents of the faith. The evidence is provided by the Church. Pope Innocent III who instigated the great crusade against the Cathars, testified on numerous occasions to the popularity of the heresy and admitted the degree to which the Catholic Church was menaced. The Inquisitional records reveal quite clearly the widespread nature of Catharism. Villages are described as wholly occupied by heretics. There is no doubt whatever that the Inquisitors regarded themselves as confronted with a formidable opposition. Pope Innocent castigated frankly and without reservations the corruption and neglect of duty on the part of the Catholic clergy whose defects he regarded as an invitation to heresy.

There were Catholic churches in which Mass had not been said for thirty years. Catholic priests, inert in the performance of their duties, had other gainful occupations and some were employed in commerce. They lived gluttonously and in flagrant concubinage. The Archbishop of Narbonne existed for years in a state of adipose inertia without setting foot in his diocese and disregarded the threats emanating from the Vatican. It must be emphasised that these are not the findings of Cathar propaganda but were openly admitted by the Papacy. When St. Dominic embarked on a preaching mission years before the formation of the Inquisition he was careful to travel sparsely and without ostentation and to ape the simplicity of the Cathar priests. The people had become all too accustomed to a Catholic priesthood living and travelling in great opulence and neglectful of its spiritual duties.

CHAPTER TWO

What was this heresy which aroused the frenzy of the Vatican and for the extermination of which the Inquisition was forged in 1233? Its basic tenets were threefold. Forces of good and evil existed in the universe from the beginning and would do so to the end. The emphasis is on the words 'in the universe' and 'from the beginning.' One can say with some justification that the Catholic Church believed also in forces of good and evil but the orthodox implication is very clearly that evil entered the heart of man after the Fall, and after his appearance on this earth. To the orthodox Christian evil was a conspiracy conducted between man and the Devil after the creation of the world. The radical difference in the Cathar conception of creation is shown by the second basic principle, that this world was created by a lower entity, called the Devil, Satan or Lucifer. The classical version of this Cathar belief was that the world was created by Jehovah, the God of the old Testament who, to the Cathars, was synonymous with the Devil. The third fundamental principle was that man possessed an immortal soul which entered matter on conception and which was purified by successive reincarnations.

As well as these three basic essentials of belief there were certain secondary articles of faith. The Cathars were essentially non-violent. To them the taking of life in war, or even in the process of justice, amounted to murder. This enlightened outlook, similar to what is called advanced opinion in these days, was accompanied by a refusal to eat animal flesh. The Cathars were vegetarians except that the consumption of fish was permitted, for reasons which are not quite clear. It has been said that this exception was due to the method of propagation commonly adopted by fishes. Possibly the fact that the fish was an especially Christian symbol made it more acceptable to the Cathars.

In addition to being vegetarians the Cathars are described as being addicted to regular fasting. Some of their periods of abstinence are said to have been long and heroic. It is quite clear that their asceticism in this respect has been ludicrously exaggerated. It has been solemnly stated that, in addition to fasts on certain days in the week, and what is more fasts based on a vegetarian diet, some of the Cathars fasted for forty days three times a year. Such statements are completely untenable. Few people ordinarily constituted could survive such a *régime*. Certainly the Cathars were no ordinary people but it is quite certain that the degree to which they abstained from food has been grossly exaggerated.

When one adds to the fasting and vegetarianism of the Cathars the necessity for absolute chastity it would seem that we are dealing with an impossibly unworldly organisation asking more of men than they can possibly fulfill. How could the peasant in the fields do a day's work and at the same time practice the asceticisms required of the Cathars? Why was the Languedoc one of the most populous areas of Europe if absolute chastity was required of its inhabitants? How could the sympathisers with Catharism fight for it in the wars against de Montfort if non-violence was expected of them? This brings us to one of the most cardinal features of Catharism without which we cannot understand its nature. The basic beliefs of Catharism in the two forces of good and evil, in reincarnation, and that the world was created by the Devil, were for all. The practices of Catharism, that is to say absolute chastity, non-violence and vegetarianism, were for the priesthood alone. Seven centuries of ludicrous misrepresentation of Catharism arises from the simple inability to distinguish between what was required of the priesthood, called Parfaits, and what was expected of the ordinary believers, or croyants. Put in the simplest terms the Cathar priesthood was recruited from a special kind of man, or woman. What they professed and achieved was not expected of the run of the mill sympathisers. To be logical the term Cathar should only be applied to the priesthood, whose functions were radically different from those of their Roman contemporaries and more to be compared with the wise men of antiquity and

7

the sages and oracles of classical Greece. It is probable that the number of Parfaits at no time exceeded four thousand. The Parfaits were a highly trained *élite* to a degree and in a manner not achieved by the priesthood of any sect in the history of modern Europe.

What were the origins of Catharism? It should be made clear at the outset that this latter phrase is merely the thirteenth century meridional name for an ancient philosophy called Dualism. The latter name derives from the belief in the two principles of good and evil. This philosophy is indefinably ancient. To some extent it is an inevitable response of man to the forces of nature. In all its forms Dualism is permeated by the conception of Light and Dark as representative of good and evil. To man in a primitive state light was not merely a symbol but in itself good because it enabled him to hunt for his food or, when he ceased to be nomadic and became a cave dweller, to cultivate his patch of earth. The night coming, when no man could work and when his enemies could steal on him from the shadows, was essentially evil. In an early stage of man's philosophical evolution it must have been easier to conceive of forces of good and evil than to think of gods, goddesses and devils as dispensers of good and evil. It is easier for us to think of God because, as a result of the increased development of our egocentric personalities, we must of necessity personalise the gods we worship and the devils we evade. At this moment of time we are crossing a watershed which leads us away from the conception of personalised gods to our perception, largely lost for centuries, of the vibrational energies of good and evil.

Some of the elements of Dualism are recognisable in European philosophy as early as the sixth century B.C. Pythagoras states clearly his belief in an immortal psyche purifying itself by a cycle of lives. He was also a vegetarian and insistent that the aspirant to higher states of consciousness should not consume animal flesh. Plato believed in reincarnation and had other Dualist leanings. There are more than hints of Dualism in some of the classical writers such as Epictitus and Democritus intervening between Pythagoras and Plato. The vexed question as to the nature of primitive Christianity cannot be

8

dealt with appropriately at this juncture. The Gnostic fathers are saturated with Dualism, particularly in so far as the latter deals with the creation of this world and the universe. A good deal of Cathar philosophy is concerned with fallen angels deriving from aeons which have strayed too far from a central source and have become contaminated by the shadow of matter. There are parts of Cathar theology, closely allied to the concepts of mysticism, which are both poetic and compatible with the findings of modern physics. There is a great deal of Dualism in the teachings of Origen and of the Syrian Gnostics and the Essenes. Later still much of the teaching of the Neoplatonists was tinged with Dualism, as witness the work of Plotinus, Porphyry and Iamblichus. Members of the Alexandrian School, such as Basilides and Valentinus, are also to a greater or lesser degree exponents of Dualism.

In the previous paragraphs I have referred to the scattered and fragmentary philosophical basis of Dualism as manifested in Europe and on the shores of the Mediterranean. It is necessary to realise that this faith had been established in Asia long before the advent of Christ. The purists debate as to whether the ancient Zoroastrianism of Persia was truly Dualist. There can be no doubt that the cult of Mithras which arose out of it, as a kind of Protestant revolt against orthodoxy, was unmistakeably Dualist. Belief in reincarnation and in forces of good and evil are undoubtedly recognisable in Mithraic practice. It is less clear as to whether the cult accepted that the world was created by a lower entity. The cult of Mithras preceded Christianity and endured to be persecuted by it after the faith of Christ had been accepted as the official religion of the Roman Empire. Mithraic practice was continued in secret after it had become anathema to the secular and clerical authorities of the Roman Empire. It was practised in the caves of the Ariège in the Languedoc, which later became centres for Cathar initiation and study. There is a tendency for the different forms of Dualism to inherit each others' places of worship. This is because Dualism is concerned with the emanatory capacity of men, places and atmospheres and recognises an ambiance which has been favourable to it in the past.

After the cult of Mithras had gone underground there occurred what is almost certainly the most widespread manifestation of Dualism the world has seen. This was attributable to Manes, who preached the three classic principles of Dualism and was flayed alive for his pains. The tide of Manicheism swept over the most civilised regions of Europe. It was also well known and established in pockets of the more backward areas of the north and west. In addition it had an immense influence on the south shores of the Mediterranean, in Asia Minor and as far east as Mongolia and India. It had the distinction of being persecuted at one and the same time by the Mongolians, the Zoroastrians in Persia, and the Christians in Europe, Asia Minor and North Africa. It revealed the constant Dualist division between the Perfecti and the ordinary believers. This has been magnified by its traducers in the assertion that the priests demanded of their flock an idolatrous reverence. This is nonsense and derives from the fact that those sympathetic to the faith of Manes made, like the Cathar croyants who were their spiritual descendants, a simple genuflexion on encountering a priest.

The word Manichean had such a dark and sinister significance that its reverberations persisted for centuries after its disappearance in the sixth century. As late as the thirteenth century the Inquisitors were still describing the Cathar heretics as Manicheans. The Manichean creed, because of a failure to comprehend that what was required of the priest was not demanded of the believer, has been regarded for centuries as a hopelessly pessimistic free-for-all between the flesh and the spirit, a sort of Dark Ages Calvinism which outdid Calvin. This attitude persists to this day when it has become the habit of authors to use the term Manichean to describe particularly repressive attitudes towards the flesh and over-preoccupation with the existence of irreconcilable opposites.

That Augustine was a convert from Manicheism to Christianity has had a dire influence on the world's estimate of Dualism. Western society has been all too prone to accept what he said about it. In addition to his misinterpretation of its nature and import his guilt at having adhered to it at one time induced

10

in him a hate which has influenced so many Catholic authorities who, throughout the centuries, have seen Dualism through his eyes and have conveyed to the world a perverted impression of it.

The Manichean faith was ruthlessly exterminated and, with few exceptions, its writings destroyed. This undesirable consummation is the common lot of Dualism. Nevertheless this resilient philosophy came to the surface again with the advent of the Paulicians who inhabited Asia Minor and were probably originally domiciled in what is modern Armenia. The Paulicians were so called because one of their original founders bore the name of Paul and because they were especially addicted to the epistles and other writings of the apostle of that name. The Paulicians included a number of turbulent elements addicted to war and employed often as mercenaries. It may surprise the reader that the peaceful Cathars should have had such warlike and intractable ancestors but we must again emphasise that we are discussing the main body of the Paulicians and not the elect who directed them. The ordinary croyant subscribing to the principles of Dualism should accept always the good and evil in his own heart and see it as a reflection in microcosm of the war between good and evil in the universe. Did not Goethe himself say that he had two souls at war in his heart? Is not his Faust in places unmistakably Dualist?

The Paulicians became such a problem that their rulers arranged for a mass transportation of a large proportion of their turbulent subjects to Europe. They were settled in Macedonia, chiefly in what is now recognised as Bulgaria. This colonisation occurred in the sixth century. Undoubtedly the Paulicians were the forerunners of the Bogomils. The latter are much better known to the Western reader. The name Paulician, or corruptions of it, were applied to Dualist heretics in Western Europe throughout the Middle Ages. Todd, writing as late as 1823, of the foundation of the monastery at Ashridge in the thirteenth century, described, probably erroneously, the founding monks as descended from the ancient Paulicians.

By the ninth century the Paulician belief had crystallized into the better known faith of the Bogomils. It is possible that the latter originated among dissentient monks in monasteries of the Orthodox Church in Bulgaria and Macedonia. The Bogomils adhered to the three cardinal principles of Dualism. Their beliefs were richly intermingled with folk lore and popular legend. There is some evidence that they appealed especially to a peasantry tyrannised by foreign masters and exploited by an often alien priesthood. This aspect of the matter has been greatly and inaccurately amplified by contemporary Bulgarian sources who see in the Bogomils the heroic precursors of the modern Communist state. It is a cardinal error to consider that Dualism could ever positively ally itself with any political or nationalistic movement. One can conceive of it making ceremonial obeisances to the established authority on the principle that the Devil you know is better than the Devil you don't know. One can understand it leaning towards the underdog in epochs when tyranny and corruption were particularly rife, but to the Dualist all earthly hierarchies are evil in being sustained by power, and any political bias he may seem to show is ephemeral and based on the ethical needs of the prevailing circumstances.

Dualism established itself in what is now Yugo-Slavia and especially in Bosnia, Herzegovina and Dalmatia. It is wrong to assume that in these latter areas it took the form of Bogomilism, though undoubtedly the latter may have been a great contributory influence. In these regions the Italian name Patarini* was often used. It is possible that the Bosnian Church was a separate organisation. Some years ago, in a psychic experience in which I was involved, my attention was drawn to the Nikolski gospels, a work produced in the vernacular for Bosnian heretics.

Dualism in Bosnia, Herzegovina and Dalmatia achieved what no other form of the religion had succeeded in doing. It became the official religion of a country. Under the Ban of Dalmatia it flourished in this region until the thirteenth century when

* This was an Italian name meaning ragpickers. It is said that in Northern Italy the Cathars visited often the streets frequented by the rag merchants. It is possible that they were gathering the raw material for papermaking. The Cathars and their successors established something of a corner in the manufacture of paper. Dualist signs were to be found in watermarks long after the Middle Ages.

it was persecuted out of existence at the instigation of the Vatican with the aid of the rulers of Catholic Hungary. Nevertheless the old faith persisted for centuries in remote regions and was still extant at the time of the Turkish conquest. Many Dalmations accepted conversion to Islam because they found it a more tolerant religion than Catholicism and also because the Islamic translation of conversion was sometimes political rather than religious. One became a Turk and continued to practise one's previous religious beliefs. A considerable proportion of the present Islamic inhabitants of Bosnia are not of Turkish blood but the descendants of the Dualists who accepted the outward forms of the Muslim faith. That Dualism was still practised openly as late as the fifteenth century is shown by the records of Turkish governors in this area who refer to the activities of what they call Christians. This was the term by which the Dualist Parfaits preferred to be known. It is obvious that the Turkish archives are recording the activities of what the people in the Languedoc called the Bonshommes (good men.)

There are fascinating collections of Bogomil tombs in modern Yugo-Slavia. There is a contemporary tendency to regard the ornamentation of these as determined by local tradition and family pride. This is quite untenable. Bogomil tombs I have seen have been decorated with unmistakable Dualist symbols.

It is claimed that teachers of mediaeval Dualism visited the Languedoc from the coastal towns of Dalmatia and particularly Trogir. This is more than feasible considering that Catharism first appeared in Western Europe in Northern Italy. As early as the beginning of the eleventh century Cathar heretics were being apprehended at Montforte. Was the name a sinister prediction of a worse fate to follow? Missionaries went from Italy to Orleans in which neighbourhood local Cathars were apprehended and burnt in the middle of the same century. The concentration of Catharism in the Languedoc was a later phenomenon. It was well consolidated towards the end of the twelfth century. That Catharism took root at this time, and in this area, was attributable to several factors. First of all the degree of tolerance in the Languedoc and Provence

13

was remarkably high in the Middle Ages. Elsewhere in Europe Jews lived in ghettoes where, in some countries, they remained into the twentieth century. In the Languedoc they not only were tolerated but achieved positions of eminence. They were employed at the court of Raymond the Sixth of Toulouse and were among the most influential members of the medical school at Narbonne. In the Midi Christians were in places employed as servants in Jewish households, a situation which would have been unthinkable elsewhere in Europe. The Lords of Les Baux were possibly in part of Jewish origin. Their family crest incorporated the star of David.

The influence of Arab physicians and poets was still clearly discernable in this area. The curious and premature multi-racial attitude of the Midi is enshrined in its literature. The basic theme of the classic Aucassin and Nicolette is that Aucassin, a product of the Midi, is threatened with hell if he chooses Nicolette who was nurtured by the Saracens and held to be contaminated by their blood. In a famous passage Aucassin expresses his preference for hell and Nicolette and his rejection of the priests and of those seeking the consolations of Christianity.

A civilisation can often be measured by its treatment of women. In the Languedoc it was possible for women, married as well as single, to own property in their own right. This is astonishing when one considers that the Married Women's Property Act was only passed in 1882. In France an equivalent measure had to await the advent of De Gaulle. This extraordinarily early manifestation of the emancipation of women was to be expected in a region where the troubadours were engaged in raising the social and spiritual stature of the sex. This progressive attitude was more directly attributable to Catharism where women were fully accepted for the priesthood. The researches of Duvernoy show us that till 1209 the ordination of women almost equalled that of men. It is only in recent decades that a few women have been ordained as deaconnesses in the Non-comformist Churches. The resistance to priestesses in the ritualistic churches is persistent and at times laughable. No woman as yet functions as a priest in Britain in the Anglican or

Roman communities.

This atmosphere of tolerance and sophistication was well suited to the implantation of Catharism which was also fortunate in another particular. The Languedoc and the foothills of the Pyrenees had a tradition of heresy. The Visigoths who not only swept over but settled in that area were devoted Aryans. The town of Castelnaudary is said to derive its name from its construction as an Aryan fortress. The early Priscillian heresy flourished in the Pyrenees. Before the advent of avowed Catharism the antipapal preacher Peter Buis and his followers, called the Petrobusians, affected this area. Peter was burnt as a heretic. His mantle was inherited by Henry of le Mans who settled in Toulouse and fulminated against the Papacy.

But of all the factors favourable to the establishment of Catharism in the Languedoc the attitude of the ruling classes was most important. Elsewhere in France the itinerant Cathar preacher had nowhere to lay his head. The situation was radically different in the Languedoc. The literate and sophisticated gentry were predominantly anti-clerical. Raymond the Sixth of Toulouse was not only tolerant of, but favourably disposed to, Catharism and took a Cathar priest with him whenever he went on a journey. The wife of the Count of Foix bore his six children following which they parted by mutual consent and she became a woman priestess or Parfaite. Roger Trencavel, Viscount of Carcassonne and Béziers, had for tutor the avowed heretic Bernard de Saissac. We cannot be sure of the exact nature of Trencavel's religious beliefs but that he was a heroic defender of the rights of heretics is beyond question. Guiraud, the Catholic historian, admits that the minor nobility of the Lauragais, the densely populated area between Toulouse and Carcassonne, were almost solidly Cathar. So were the minor gentry of the Corbières, the arid eastern extremity of the Pyrenees which stretches between Carcassonne and Narbonne. Among these noble families it happened very frequently, and in the Lauragais was almost the custom, for one of the daughters to be trained as a priestess. Up to 1209, the year of the great crusade, thirty per cent of the Cathar priesthood were of noble birth. This infiltration by the favoured

15

classes into the priesthood is one of the unique features of Catharism.

Catharism was also strong among the rich merchants and the professional classes. The practical influence of these sections of society was considerable. In its sociological structure the Languedoc was at least three hundred years before its time. The privileged bourgeoisie recruited from the merchants and lawyers played a considerable role in the government of Toulouse. They were elected as Consuls to a city council which resembled a little the political structure of the Roman republic. Their power was enhanced by the fact that Toulouse had a citizen army to which the merchant class contributed considerably.

It is necessary to note another important factor in the political structure of the Languedoc. The Cathars concerned themselves with the establishment of a class of skilled tradesmen. The Parfaits supervised and themselves shared in the labour of workshops in which men were trained in leather and paper-making and in the textile trade. (Catharism has been described as an astonishing amalgam of mysticism and common sense.) What should also be added is that, however much they merited the term mystic, they were ferocious workers. Because of their interest in these primitive industries the Cathars helped in the foundation of an instructed artisan class which was strongly impregnated with Catharism.

Catharism was strongest in the sophisticated and progressive atmosphere of the towns and cities. There can be no greater error than to regard it as a nebulous creed appealing, on the one hand, to heroic but uncritical missionaries, and on the other to simple, dogged and often superstitious peasants. Nevertheless it was also widespread through the country districts. Frequently the Inquisition described whole villages and certain country regions as totally contaminated. It was obstinately rooted in what is now the department of the Ariège. Its last clandestine concentration at the end of the thirteenth century was in the remote valleys of the upper Ariège.

The anticlericalism which began in the higher echelons of society filtered down to the lower orders. A common retort to an accusation the individual considered unjust was, 'What do you take me for, a priest?' There can be no doubt that the corruption, licentiousness and inertia of the Roman clergy of those days contributed to an anticlericalism already well rooted in those favoured and sophisticated regions. This latter tendency was also inflamed by a considerable proportion of the Troubadour poets who were to add distinction to their age by being the fathers of European poetry. A particular variety of poem called the Sirventes was dedicated to the denigration of the Catholic clergy. No anti-clerical propaganda produced in France at the end of the nineteenth and the beginning of the twentieth century could equal in vituperation and contempt what had been written by such troubadours as Pierre Cardenal seven hundred years previously.

In the early years of the thirteenth century the weather would seem to have been set fair for Catharism. For a start its theology had been ironed out and unified at the conference at St. Felix de Caraman in 1167. Till that date there had been in the Languedoc two varieties of Catharism, the absolute and the mitigé. The division between the two rested on a number of theological subtleties but the main point at issue was the varying versions of the fall of man. In absolute Catharism the Fall occurred early in the creation. A number of dissentient aeons were seduced by the attraction of form and matter. One of these became the fallen angel who created the world. In other words the evil impulse dedicated to the creation of form occurred *before* the creation of this world. Evil therefore clearly pre-existed before the construction of this planet. For the most part Catharism mitigé regarded evil as entering into the nature of created man after his appearance on earth. Metaphorically speaking it is the difference between the Fall occurring in heaven or in the first Eden. It will be seen that in the matter of the creation Catharism mitigé is not far from the teachings of orthodox Catholicism, though of course belief in reincarnation and in the existence of the two principles renders the two faiths completely independent of each other. In actual fact, at the end of the twelfth and at the beginning of the thirteenth century, there were in the Languedoc supposedly orthodox Catholic

17

ecclesiastics who taught a mixture of Catholicism and Catharism. For the most part the Cathars and the generality of Catholic priests were on good terms with each other. This was in accordance with the urbane tradition of the Languedoc. It was only with the intervention of Pope Innocent III, de Montfort and the Northern lords, and later of the Inquisition and the French crown, that a persistent hatred alien to the ambiance of the Languedoc was injected into the procedures.

The two forms of Catharism persisted in Italy long after the battle had been gained for the absolute variety in the Languedoc. In Italy there were separate centres for the two varieties, each of which had its own priests and bishops.

The council at which the Languedoc devoted itself to absolute Catharism was held at the instigation of Nicetas, a priest from the Balkans where Dualism was rife. The fact that he should have been called in as an authority shows how close the Bogomils and the Bosnian heresy were to Catharism. Nicetas has been described by Catholic writers as a kind of secret pope of Catharism. This is completely erroneous and derives from the fact that in the Balkan churches the word pope was synonymous with priest.

The simple hierarchy of the Cathar church was outlined at the council of St Felix de Caraman. There were four Bishoprics at Toulouse, Carcassonne, Albi and Agen. The number of bishops never rose to more than five. A fifth bishopric was established at Razes in 1225 to minister to the needs of the considerable population in the country between Carcassonne and Toulouse. It is not entirely clear why the Cathars ever became known as Albigensians. The idea that the name was derived from alba, white, signifying chastity, is entirely without foundation. The name Albigeois signifies the country round the town of Albi where it is evident that Catharism was strongly implanted. There is no evidence that its adherents there were any more numerous than in Toulouse or Carcassonne. Perhaps it was the earliest centre from which Catharism radiated.

Each bishop was served by a filius major and minor. The former succeeded to the bishopric on the death of the bishop. The filius minor became a filius major. The office of deacon represented a higher grade than an ordinary Parfait. From the ranks of the deacons the filii minor and major were elected. There were no archbishops and no hierarchical superstructure. The bishops were responsible for their flocks in their particular area and none was senior to the other.

CHAPTER THREE

What was the threat offered to the Catholic Church on the eve of the Great Crusade of 1209? (This was actually not the first crusade against the Cathars. An earlier foray under Henry de Marsiac had occurred in 1181. It was of relatively brief duration but of dire significance, if the Languedoc had read the omens rightly.) Firstly the two most advanced civilisations of Europe, those of the Languedoc and Northern Italy, were largely given over to heresy. In the first the ruling classes were overwhelmingly, and in the latter considerably, on the side of the heretics. Even in terms of temporal power there was a danger of a breakaway. Already in the anticlerical Languedoc there were regions where the disaffected nobility had seized Church property. This would have been extremely unlikely elsewhere in Europe and in most regions unthinkable. In some of the larger Italian towns like Turin the Cathar sympathisers dominated the city councils.

Apart from these temporal threats there was also to be considered the menace to ecclesiastical privilege. As reincarnationists the Cathars rejected the doctrine of grace. Men purified themselves by successive incarnations and not in virtue of a mysterious gift called grace bestowed by a personalised God and dispensed in graduated doses by a priesthood in the form of absolutions, penances and the usual offertories. The Cathars denied the efficacy of the sacraments recognised by the Church. Baptism, marriage and the Eucharist were equally excluded. This was a shattering blow at the privileges and powers of the Roman priesthood. It denied the right of the infant to qualify for salvation by a ceremony presided over by the priest. This was not merely a question of the removal of a privilege, though this deprival of a traditional perquisite counted for something among the more corrupt representatives of the priesthood. But to the devoted priest the denial of the efficacy of such a sacrament as baptism questioned the very reason of his being and of his sacred function. In being ordained he had been granted the right of issuing passports to salvation and banging the doors of heaven not only on unbelievers and heretics but on the unbaptised. It is useless for us to consider this matter from the standpoint of modern libertarian Catholicism which recognises that the emancipation of the sinner can be achieved without constant attendance at Mass and without a scrupulous observance of the other sacraments and obligations. In the Middle Ages the latter were paramount for salvation and the purity and ethical blamelessness of the life of the individual counted for little in comparison with his observance of the rules of the Church. This is shown clearly by the remarkable regularity with which the Inquisitors themselves paid tribute to the blameless lives of the heretics. That the latter were nevertheless subsequently condemned is a clear indication that a life of chastity and love meant nothing set against the denial of the Church's right to confer grace by sacraments. It should be clearly understood that, except for recalcitrants and heretics and, at the opposite pole, the dregs of society, man in the Middle Ages was dominated by the fear of hell. The latter was emphasised, for the most part with complete sincerity, by the priesthood, who themselves believed in the doctrine of eternal punishment. This intense preoccupation with hell was treated by a prescription of ritualistic observances conducted in an atmosphere of awe which was a subtle mixture of reverence and fear. It is not the first time in history that obsessional states have been marked and controlled by ritualistic observance. The practice has spilt over into lay pathology.

The Cathar attitude to the Eucharist was a crucial issue. It was not merely that they alleged that its importance was exaggerated. The Vaudois, practitioners of a heresy contemporary with Catharism, insisted that the good life and the direct practice of the word of Christ was equal to, or even of greater merit than, the reception of the sacraments. In this the Vaudois were precursors of the different variations of the Reformed Church, and in particular the Waldensians. But though Protestantism, and particularly Non-Conformity, was to devalue Holy Communion in relation to the Catholic Mass and, on the whole, to celebrate it less frequently, it remains to this day a sacred and significant sacrament. Catharism on the other hand denied altogether the usefulness of orthodox Christian sacraments. It went further and indicated that the Eucharist was pagan, a kind of depraved magic and basically evil. To their remarkably sophisticated intelligence it derived from the old myth that the king must die for his people who gained strength from eating his flesh and drinking his blood. The doctrine of transubstantiation, that Christ was actually incorporated in the consecrated bread and wine, was utterly incomprehensible to Catharism which insisted that the son of God was not incarnate in the flesh. This being so it was inconceivable that Christ, in his true nature, had perished on the cross and, equally, that he was able to reappear in the bread and wine.

The Cathar rejection of the Eucharist is an illustration of the enormous gulf which exists between those for whom religion involves the practice of magic and those for whom it is excluded. It is hard for members of ritualistic Churches to accept that what to them is sacred is a form of ancient magic comparable to what has been, and still is, practised in some primitive religions. But surely the belief that concrete articles such as bread and wine can be transformed by a form of words into vehicles conferring enormous spiritual sustenance on their recipients is a form of magic or at least analagous to it? We never regard as magic what is sacred to us. We prefer to regard as superstition what other people reverence. This is not saying that for all Anglicans or Roman Catholics the Eucharist has necessarily some profound occult significance. Equally one is not insisting that its influence is illusory or even nefarious. The relevant issue is that there is a huge gulf between those who believe that ritualistic practices contribute to our spiritual development and those for whom the latter demands a more direct contact with a supreme being or force of goodness, plus the determination to haul ourselves up by our own shoe strings.

To deny the efficacy of the Eucharist must have been genuinely horrifying both to the Catholic priest and the simple believer. To the former the Cathar was questioning his right and his capacity to save souls and with that his whole raison d'être. To the more cynical and corrupt members of the priesthood the challenge to their more earthly privileges was paramount. This same motive may have operated at the subconscious level in priests not especially corrupt, but one must allow that a considerable mass of priests were genuinely terrified at the challenge to beliefs which, however misguided they may appear by modern standards, were genuinely held and, as it were, mixed with their archetypes. To the more rabid believers denial of the efficacy of the sacraments was both terrifying and exasperating. It implied that hell was still round the corner and also that, in receiving the sacraments of the Church, he had taken erroneous and insufficient steps for its avoidance. This must have posed a terrifying problem for the fervent and superstitious believer. It must be accepted that, by contemporary standards, most unprivileged believers in the Middle Ages, justified the use of these adjectives. But in the relatively civilised and sophisticated atmosphere of the Languedoc the situation was different. The Cathars had removed largely from the people the fear of hell. This was perhaps their most significant contribution to the emancipation of common man. Not to understand this is to fail to realise that Catharism was not only an enlightened but an optimistic creed. Some of the contemporary defenders of Catharism, particularly in Britain and other North Temperate zone countries, regard Catharism as a dour, Calvinistic and basically pessimistic religion. Sir Steven Runciman who is, on the whole, very fair in his assessment of the Cathars, regards the religion as foredoomed because of its built-in pessimism. Those holding such views are at a loss to explain how such a repressive and pessimistic creed could have spread like wildfire through the most sophisticated and sceptical region of Europe and, in the case of the Languedoc and Provence, in an area where les moeurs were considerably lighter than elsewhere. It should be noted that Catharism was often strong in those regions where the Courts of Love flourished.

The crucial issue was that, to the Cathars, life on this planet was hell. They believed that the world was created by Satan, or at least by a lower entity. They regarded it as the lowest plane of consciousness to which we sink. Though they were too enlightened to think of hell as a spatial concept, this world was, in terms of torture and, in particular, of unmerited torture, its nearest equivalent. The Cathars believed that the statement that Christ descended into hell meant that he came, of his own free will, to what was virtually its equivalent. One can readily understand how any sharp witted peasant in the Languedoc could embrace enthusiastically a creed which regarded this world as hell. Such a view explained for him the inequalities and injustices under which he laboured, though these were far less so in the Languedoc than elsewhere. It helped, indeed, to develop a political awareness and a recognition of his own rights, attitudes already foreshadowed on the practical plane by the workshops provided by the Cathars and, on the intellectual, by the constant instruction he received from the inveterate and well-read Cathar preachers whose erudition was such that, in the days of persecution, heresy was expected of those who were particularly well-versed in the scriptures. Most of all, if this world were hell, there were always compensations. There was sunshine, fertile earth, a plethora of fêtes. The nobility of the Languedoc and Provence had a penchant for visual spectacles allied often to a talent for bankruptcy. There were also wine, women and song. If this was hell it had its compensations and was supportable for most of the people most of the time.

These views are contrary to those held by the avowed detractors of the Cathars, both by those who were their contemporaries and those who have continued to vilify them for more than seven hundred years. Naturally practising Catholics who were their contemporaries could not be expected to regard their doctrines with anything but repugnance. Catholic antagonists down the centuries are largely in error because their main and, in the last analysis, only source of information is the records of the Inquisition. To consult those registers for solid and unbiassed information about the Cathars is comparable to insisting that the Gestapo is the best authority to enlighten us as to the nature and practice of Jewry. The Inquisitorial records are full of information about the Cathar attitude to marriage and sex. They would lead us to suppose that the Cathars were both pathologically ascetic and hopelessly depraved, contradictions arising, as we cannot emphasise too often, from the inability to distinguish between what was expected of the Cathar Parfaits and the croyants, or ordinary believers. To this day, among the uninstructed, the Cathars are regarded as opposed to marriage, practitioners of race suicide, which presumably means birth control, sexual perverts and, particularly in their opposition to marriage, destroyers of society as a natural consequence of their being opposed to marriage and to family life. This is still the orthodox view of a number of Catholics, both in England and France, who could with justification claim to be people of reasonable culture. Only a few years ago I was told by an otherwise erudite Catholic priest that the Cathars were people with unpleasant habits and that the Church had had to suppress them. He offered me the use of a Catholic library to prove his point.

Nevertheless it is not the Catholics alone who are in error in these matters. Many Protestant writers accept the conclusions reached about the above mentioned aspects of Catharism. The findings of some are based simply on a 'there is no smoke without fire' attitude. The son of a Protestant missionary and himself a classical scholar of some distinction, a fact which should have attracted him to Catharism in view of the latter's Platonic aspects, told me that of all the heresies which had been persecuted Catharism merited most the treatment it had received. To do him justice I think he was probably less concerned with the Cathars' hypothetical sexual delinquencies than with the equally hypothetical repressive puritanism attributed to them. Many of the Protestant, or at any rate non-Catholic writers most warmly appreciative of Catharism, and who refer to it as a noble and grossly maltreated creed, are puzzled and hurt by certain aspects of Catharism which remain mysterious for them. Why were so many Cathar believers, not Parfaits, who lived at Montségur in the years of the siege, described as having their concubines with them? While allowance should always be made for the Inquisitional tendency to use derogatory terms it is clear that there was more to it than this and that the Cathar

25

attitude to the sacrament of marriage needs special consideration. It is an absolutely vital issue to the student of Catharism. Most of the assessments of it in the past have been erroneous to the point of banality.

In discussing Catharism it is necessary to divest ourselves completely of the idea that this was a mediaeval heresy essentially incomprehensible to modern man. For a start it was more than a heresy. It was a comprehensive and lucid philosophy of enormous scope and considerable antiquity. It is perhaps reasonable to infer that modern man can never put himself in the shoes of any of his mediaeval precursors. This is a safe but not entirely accurate description. The beliefs and attitudes of Cathars were remarkably modern. We have seen this already in our consideration of the different aspects of their cult of non-violence. Their attitude to marriage was remarkably contemporary.

The Cathars were hostile to the sacrament of, but strongly in favour of, the institution of marriage. They could not accept that marriages were made in heaven and that the fate of lovers joined in wedlock depended on grace descending on them during the wedding ceremony. They did not believe that sexual contact was sinful and taboo until the hour of wedlock and that afterwards what was illicit and sordid became in some way sanctified. Does even the most devoted modern Anglican truly believe what is so confidently stated in the marriage service? Is the marriage ceremony a sacrament ordained by God and does the Anglican seriously regard it as a young people's licence to copulate? Is it seriously believed that it is the responsibility of God and the Church that the young appear virgin at the altar but that afterwards, by a rapid amendment of official policy, they should take good care to reproduce their kind? The Cathars insisted that the sexual urge was basically the same before and after marriage and that it could not be disinfected or damned in the course of a short ceremony.

The idea that Catharism was against marriage was, even in the thirteenth century, completely ludicrous. The huge proportion of those sympathetic to it were married in Catholic churches because there was no other recognised alternative and

26

because, for the majority, marriage has, from time immemorial, required a ritual celebration. Even in this permissive age a majority of those intending to live together still opts for some kind of ceremony. Certainly the Cathars did not look askance on those among their more fervent believers who, genuinely in love with each other, opted to live together without benefit of clergy. A minority embarked on such joint establishments with the blessing of the Parfaits. The latter were prepared to conduct a simple service which joined them together. This, in its simplicity, was a forerunner of the civil marriage but is not to be considered as of the same nature because the Cathars were in no sense allied to any secular authority, though prepared to consort with it under special circumstances. Among those described by the Inquisition as living with their concubines were many who existed as man and wife, who were faithful to each other, and who had enjoyed the blessing of the Parfaits and undergone the ceremony conducted by them.

It is quite obvious that the accusation that the Cathars were against marriage was to a large extent something thought up by their traducers after they had been to all intents and purposes exterminated. Those who lived in the Languedoc in the twelfth and thirteenth centuries could see that devoted believers in Catharism continued to marry in the Catholic church and even to have their children baptised there. (How many complete agnostics in our day feel uncomfortable unless their children have been baptised in a church?) A great deal of the misapprehension as to the Cathar teaching on marriage arose in the centuries after their disappearance and was derived from a non-intuitive misreading of the Inquisitorial depositions by people who failed altogether to distinguish the handful of Parfaits from the hundreds of thousands of ordinary believers. What the former said about marriage should be translated as applying only to themselves. Here the theory of antipathy to marriage wears very thin. It was absolutely distinctive of Catharism that a sizeable proportion of its priests and priestesses were recruited from those who had been married or who had lived what would nowadays be considered normal sexual lives. Esclarmonde, Countess of Foix, had six children before

27

becoming a Parfaite. Hélis de Mazerolles was the mother of Pierre de Mazerolles who was implicated in the murder of the two Inquisitors at Avignonet in 1242. Braïda de Montserver became a Parfaite after her husband had died and her son and daughter had grown up. Far from being the depressive ascetics they have been painted the Cathar priesthood preferred to recruit itself from people of mature years who had experienced the hazards of life including its physical aspects. Today we accept without reflection that Anglican and Non-conformist priests should marry. That the Parfaits should have been recruited from those who had had affairs is not strictly analogous but, when one realises that the Catholic Church still insists on celibacy, it testifies to a remarkable degree to what one can call the modern outlook of the Cathars.

It has been accepted for seven centuries that the Cathar attitude to sex was at its worst perverted and at its best so ascetic as to amount to a psychological self-mutilation. This is an important issue because no less an authority than Duvernoy insists that the attitude to sex is one of the main yardsticks by which one measures whether this or that heresy's philosophical attitude is Dualistic. The charge of practising race suicide is ludicrous. There were no signs of it in what was one of the most intensely populated and urbanised regions in Europe. From whence came the armies which fought for the defence of the Languedoc and Catharism? What could it matter to the social character of those times if a few hundred Parfaits in the Languedoc and Italy abstained from sexual intercourse, particularly when a proportion of those were only recruited to the priesthood in middle age?

The libels which have been levelled at Catharism are not only mendacious but completely irrelevant. The criticism of the Cathars is almost always of the 'heads I win tails you lose' variety. The Cathars were so unnaturally chaste that, had their example been followed, which was never and never will be remotely likely, the human race would cease to exist. At the same time such chastity was so unnatural that it must be accompanied by sexual perversion. Bonnacorsi describes the Cathars roundly as sodomites. The word bougres, derived originally from Bulgar to denote the Bogomil roots of Catharism, was later distorted in France to indicate that the Cathars were sodomites. The heretics have therefore the dubious distinction of having given rise to one of the commonest contemporary obscenities. One can argue that this, or other sexual perversions, may well have been practised by zealous croyants who misread the Cathar teaching on procreation but I do not believe there is a single clearly described case of sexual perversion in the Inquisitorial records. One could surely have relied on the Inquisitors to have reported such a matter had they encountered it. They were remarkably honest in testifying to the genuine purity of the Parfaits and their most devoted followers. This good reputation was widely disseminated among the people, so much so that one individual accused by the authorities of being a heretic denied the accusation, and defended himself on the grounds that he ate, drank and fornicated like a Catholic.

It is assumed that the Cathar attitude to marriage and sex was one of the reasons why they were held in horror by the Catholic priesthood of their day. Looking back across seven centuries it is easy to misread the situation. Is it reasonable to suppose that the Catholic Church objected to celibate priests in the Cathar community when the same requirements were expected of their own? Catholic criticism could only have been based on social rather than moral issues. It is easy to translate the Cathar antipathy to the sacrament of marriage as an attack on marriage itself and through it on the basis of society. This, indeed, is the line which has been taken in the seven centuries which have elapsed since the extermination of Catharism. I cannot believe it was the attitude assumed by their more informed Catholic contemporaries. Had the secular and clerical authorities been working hand in glove we can see that their combined authority would regard with horror any criticism of the institution of marriage. But in the Languedoc the aristocracy and the priesthood were at loggerheads. It is inconceivable that, in supporting the Cathars, the former would connive at their own destruction. It is not in the nature of ruling classes to plan their own destruction in full, waking consciousness. The question is also answered by the fact that they themselves supplied a high proportion of Parfaits. In addition the Courts of Love, admittedly more common in Provence than the Languedoc, had, for decades, made relatively light of the institution of marriage.

The accusation that the fathers were enemies of society has been continued uncritically by hindsight for centuries. Jacques Bainville, a twentieth century French historian of some repute, describes the Cathars as the Bolsheviks of the Middle Ages. Until the last three years the nature and message of Catharism has been buried beneath the interpretations and misrepresentations of centuries. Much of the evidence found in books by reputable historians is derived from single statements made by illiterate peasants under interrogation and torture. I have traced several of these, passed on from one historian to another, expressed with great confidence, bearing all the marks of authenticity, and utterly unacceptable as fact.

CHAPTER FOUR

Were there any other Cathar attitudes or practices likely to have aroused the fear and hatred of the Catholic authorities? Undoubtedly their attitude to the crucifix must have been difficult to support by those reared to venerate it and encountering it everywhere outside and inside the churches. Rejecting the Christian doctrine of the incarnation and of grace from on high it was also inevitable that the Cathars dispensed with the idea of Christ as a redeemer. To them He was a son of God and a special kind of man but not a premeditated sacrifice. The Cathars had what we would now call a truly scientific view of natural phenomena. They believed that there was every gradation between matter conceived of as inert spirit and spirit as etherealised matter. They would have well understood Schiller's dictum that God sleeps in the stone, wakes in the plant, dreams in the animal and lives in man. To them Christ had the appearance of human form but was so essentially etherealised that he was able to reveal his spiritual nature to his disciples at the transfiguration on the mount. The Inquisitors had some kind of glimmering of this concept when they described the Cathars as believing that Christ was a kind of phantom. Modern students of anthroposophy will have little difficulty in comprehending this Cathar conception. It is doubtful how much of this kind of knowledge the Cathars imparted to the general public. Essentially humble and universally compassionate they nevertheless distinguished between people living at different levels of consciousness. This kind of concept of Christ's nature was disseminated only at reunions of people with special insight. The peasant Cathar's detestation of the crucifix was expressed in cruder form. 'Would you worship the gallows your father died on?'

In what other ways did the Cathars arouse the opprobrium of

their opponents? There is always the question of the Endura. Duvernoy has shown that this was the name given to an especially prolonged fast. To the more dramatically inclined it indicates suicide by starvation. The argument runs thus. The Cathar negation of the flesh, shown naturally in their chastity and abstemious habits, reached such lengths that they encouraged men to escape from imprisonment in matter by slow suicide. This rests on evidence so flimsy as to be negligible. Most of it hinges on what followed after the administration of the Consolamentum, the only sacrament recognised by the Cathars, to the dying. In accepting the Consolamentum the recipient abjured the flesh and dedicated himself to the life of the spirit. It was administered to those of mature years who wanted to become Parfaits. These were a tiny minority. It is only human nature that the generality deferred this rite till their deathbed, and for these latter certain requirements had to be fulfilled. The case must be from the medical point of view hopeless. The patient had to understand the significance of what he was doing. A large proportion of the Parfaits were trained as doctors. All Parfaits had some knowledge of what perhaps we can call first aid. People who are moribund do not habitually ingest food and are usually fed with drops of liquid. It is obvious that the Parfaits were very skilled in deciding the time at which the patient should receive the Consolamentum. Few of the recipients took much nourishment after its administration. This was magnified by scandal and fevered over-imagination to a belief that such patients were encouraged to starve themselves to death. It is not usual for the already moribund to refuse, or to act on, advice as to self-destruction. A case is recorded of what was obviously a mistaken diagnosis. The patient received the Consolamentum, recovered against all expectations, was fed by his relatives and was not held to be bound by the sacrament which normally required that the recipient should abjure the enticements of the flesh.

In the course of centuries fanciful interpretations have been expounded to include suffocation of the dying by pillows. Why suffocate anyone who was on the way out? Opening the patient's veins has also been postulated. There is absolutely no evidence whatever that the Cathar priests, notorious for their good nature and known to the people simply as the Bonshommes (the good men), ever encouraged suicide or hastened the death of the sick. It is possible, but no more than possible, that the Endura may have been practised once or twice in the desperate last days of Catharism in the upper Ariège in the last years of the thirteenth century, but by then Catharism was in its decadence and its priests less cultivated and instructed than in the first half of the century.

Cathar priests acting as doctors were accused by the Inquisition of using their influence with their patients to spread the principles of Dualism. This is the only charge against them which was probably well-founded. They were indefatigable preachers and polemists. It is not likely that they ceased to instruct their ailing flock.

The accusation of undue asceticism levelled at the Cathars cannot surely be sustained in the face of our knowledge that so many were doctors. It is difficult to see how, at one and the same time, the individual can be engaged in the mortification of the flesh and in ministering sympathetically to the pains to which it is subject.

CHAPTER FIVE

Catharism was, like primitive Christianity, a religion of emanation. There is nothing specifically unique in Christ's message as
it has come down to us. It is profitless to suggest that before, or
for that matter since, his day no one has suggested that we
should love our neighbour as ourselves. Some time ago I read
through St. John's gospel to see if I could come any nearer to the
unique nature of Christ's message. I chose this gospel because
of the fact that it was the most mystical. It was years since I had
studied any of the gospels carefully. I was astonished to find
that in this, written by the disciple who had known Jesus best,
the evangelist was so concerned with what manner of man Jesus
was and with the miracles he performed. It is clear that what
was unique about Christ was his extraordinary emanatory capacity. When he asked Matthew to leave the seat of custom the
evangelist did so not because of the particular quality of
Christ's message but because of the compulsion of his presence.
Christ was distinguished above all others by what we would
now call his psychic capacities. His gift of healing was so developed that he could raise the dead.* He was also clairvoyant, as
witness his conversation with the woman by the well. Christ
was, in fact, a special kind of being in whom what we would
now call extrasensory capacities were intensely developed.
That his spiritual endowments were also immense is beyond
question but we are at the moment only concerned with his psychic capacities.

* I cannot accept the rationalist or modern churchman's view that Christ's
miracles were performed only on the unstable and suggestible and that the
physical diseases he is supposed to have treated were in fact hysterical conditions simulating organic maladies. I know for certain of a distinguished orthodox consultant who was cured of cancer by psychic healing. I have no
difficulty in accepting that Christ could also achieve what was accomplished
by a woman in Somerset in 1974.

Now Christ insisted that his gifts were not peculiar to himself but should be possible to his disciples. In other words he believed himself able to ignite them by his own emanation so that they could emulate his feats of healing. This is clearly laid down in the injunction to the primitive Christians that they should not only preach the word but heal the sick. This particular recommendation is absolutely unique in world religions. The Buddhist and Moslem may be required to be compassionate to the sick but it is not laid fairly and squarely on their shoulders that they should practise healing. It is recorded in the *Acts* and elsewhere in the *New Testament* that the disciples carried out Christ's wishes. This implies that at that time the practitioners of Christianity had developed some of his emanatory capacity which was revealed in healing and in other extra-sensory manifestations. It is clear that Christ acted as a catalyst in arousing the healing powers of those with whom he was associated and that these in their turn ignited others. The process of divine ignition seems to have continued till the third century A.D. During this period there appears to have been a number of people especially gifted, even to the degree that their potentialities and accomplishments approximated to those of Christ. The Empress Julia, aiming at a syncretic religion, tried to elevate one of these prophets and healers, Apollonius of Tyre, to the level of a Christ figure.

Early Christianity was, in fact, an intensely spiritist religion. For centuries the Church has disregarded almost totally the injunction to heal and has only recently resumed its responsibilities, perfunctorily at first, and now with a certain desperation, because it has been forced to do so by the resurgence of interest in natural healing, that is to say healing achieved without the aid of the techniques and appurtenances of official medicine. Now in the thirteenth century the pattern of primitive Christianity was exactly reproduced. Here again we had a limited number of men and women endowed with extraordinary emanatory capacity. The extra-sensory talents of the Parfaits were recognised by the Inquisitors who attributed their powers to witchcraft. In reading some of the depositions made to the Inquisition it is often difficult to decide whether the defendant is being accused of heresy, or witch-craft. It has been suggested, and very appropriately, that the Parfaits acted often as mediums. There can be no doubt whatever of their healing capacity. This involved not only expert and remarkably contemporary knowledge of medicines as they occur in nature. Potions made of rose hips or sloes in a wine base were used to combat infections and as tonics. Dr. Twenty-man, physician to the Royal Homoeopathic Hospital, London, tells me that a preparation made from sloes is still the most efficacious tonic in debilitated states. The Cathars anticipated penicillin by the use of moulds to combat infections. These measures are classifiable as orthodox medicine but in addition they practised the laying on of hands. It was largely through this latter technique that their psychic power and emanatory capacity was manifested.

The laying on of hands as practised by the Parfaits was something inherited from primitive Christianity. It was in no sense a generalised benediction plus the relaxing effect induced by contact with those who had the gift of healing in their fingers. It was a sophisticated, comprehensive and scientifically based system of healing. The hands were kept still at certain fixed points. The latter were established in relation to certain bony areas. Treatment to a diseased tissue or organ involved placing one hand over the affected area and the other on one of the fixed points, not necessarily the nearest. In cardiac disease one hand could be placed over the heart and the other at a certain point near the thumb. An alternative method was to place the hands on the nearest points at either side of the affected area. A person with an abscess on the forearm could be treated by hands placed at specifically indicated sites at the thumb or elbow of the same side. This geographical siting of the hands was a basic feature of the technique but the possession of healing power by the therapist was absolutely essential.

One had in Catharism the same pattern as that revealed in primitive Christianity, a limited number of individuals with special gifts preaching the word, healing the sick and igniting a number of others with the capacity to do so. I say a number of others because the contemporary idea that everybody can heal

36

if they only realise their potentialities is unfortunately inaccurate. One cannot explain why a body of people endowed with these special gifts should have reassembled in the Languedoc. Certainly there are periods in history when the materialism of a disturbed world is offset by an enhanced spirituality on the part of a minority. This happened in and around the fifth century B.C., witness Buddha, Heraclitus, Lao Tse and Confucius. It happened also at the birth of Christ and again in the thirteenth century. The aspect of place must also be considered because different combinations of earth, air and water are conducive, to varying degrees, to psychic activity. The Pyrenees has always been a breeding ground for those favouring the direct, mystical approach to God and reality. Areas of the Middle East have specialised in the production of good and false prophets.

This psychic, emanatory capacity of the Parfait cannot be exaggerated. Years ago Sir Steven Runciman said, with commendable prescience, that for many the way back to Catharism appears to be by way of the occult. This has certainly been so in my experience. I have made no attempt to communicate with discarnate Cathar entities. They have been at pains to re-establish contact with me by a dovetailed and beautifully logical process of communication which I have described elsewhere. It was made clear to me that, after seven centuries, I should do all I could to spread, in writing and verbally, the knowledge of Catharism. I was not encouraged to missionise in a sectarian manner on behalf of a heresy of limited scope. I learnt that Dualism, of which Catharism was the last openly and widely asserted example, is the oldest established philosophy in the world, that its truths have persisted, often in secret and known only to a few, through centuries of persecution and that in Europe itself there has been a continuous and unbroken tradition of Dualism for at least three millennia. It was made clear to me that the purpose behind the dissemination of knowledge of Catharism was to resist, so far as is in our power, the engulfing tide of materialism. The discarnate entities insisted that in terms of human destiny the hour is five minutes before midnight and that it is necessary to disseminate knowledge so that the latter will persist if necessary through another dark age. As a doctor and psychiatrist I was enabled to see by Braïda de Montserver, dead in 1241, and by others of her kind, that in medicine it was not necessary to distinguish between what can be achieved by orthodox medicine and what by healing. It was not a question of my recognising the limits of orthodox medicine because, to me, to be a doctor is to emphasise merely one facet of cosmic knowledge. Doctor is, or should be, merely the name given to one aspect of the complete man. We are not here to choose between orthodox medicine and this or that cult of healing. What has been made clear beyond any doubt is that the Cathar medicine of the thirteenth century, with its skilled knowledge of drugs, its use of hypnosis to induce anaesthesia before the treatment of wounds, its relaxing techniques and its canalisation of the therapeutic energy of goodness in the laying on of hands, represented a complete system of medicine the like of which had not been seen in Europe since Greek medicine was practised in temples, and running water, massage and music used as therapeutic accessories.

This psychic emanatory capacity was such as to break through the barriers of seven centuries as well as through my own scepticism. That I should have received these communications is something I could not have imagined even six years ago. At the time I wrote *The Cathars and Reincarnation*, while I accepted completely the validity of Mrs. Smith's revelations, I had no idea that I was being approached for a set purpose. It is clear from their capacity to annihilate time and to communicate with us across seven centuries, that these Cathar Parfaits were, to say the least, unusual people. This leads us to what is the essential core of this book. The Parfaits were especially selected for their psychic gifts, and because of their capacity to emanate the energy of goodness. It is not without significance that their goodness was universally commented on even by their adversaries and that they earned the name 'the good men'.

The nature of selection of the Parfaits was laborious, careful and intensely scientific. It included meditation on different phrases and objects and the completing of mandalas. The latter is an Eastern technique of which we have been reminded by Jung and Wilhelm, but seven centuries ago the Cathars used it to give insight into the nature and potentialities of those who wished to be Parfaits. Nowadays we would call this kind of thing typological testing. It was used for two purposes, firstly, to separate the sheep from the goats and to discover those who were trainable as Parfaits and, secondly, to reveal what were the particular aptitudes of the persons selected for the priesthood. Some were especially destined for preaching, others for scholarship, others as seers, prophets and students of philosophy, a large number as technicians in the Cathar workshops and, larger than any other category, those to be trained as healers. To heal was part of the heart and core of Cathar practice. It was for this reason that a large number of the Parfaits were women. The Cathars recognised that healing power is more common in women, a fact repeatedly disputed by a minority of men but born out by observation of those engaged in healing over centuries. In addition the classically feminine attributes of intuition, compassion and above all passivity naturally dispose them to act as instruments of healing.

It will be seen that the recruitment to the Cathar priesthood was totally different from anything we have experienced in modern Europe, if we define the latter as the civilisation following the disappearance of the classical age with the downfall of the Roman Empire. In the Languedoc of the thirteenth century the Roman priesthood was recruited from those with a genuine vocation, from others with a taste for theology and ritual, and from others attracted by the prospect of self-advancement. The Roman Church at this time was the poor man's opportunity. Men elected to study for the priesthood at an early age while they were still addicted to the plethora of ideas which is the intoxication of youth. The situation has not greatly changed in the Christian Churches in the last seven centuries. The point at issue is that entrants were for the most part young men, inexperienced in life, and intellectually attracted to a particular system of theology. Being human beings they were good, bad and indifferent but, most of all, they were received because of their intellectual homage to a particular system of verbal conceptions. The Cathars were elected according to the type of men and women they were. Their capacity to make psychic contact with others and to emanate creatively counted more than their addiction to theology. (The basic principles of Catharism were simple enough.) It was also preferred of candidates that they had first lived ordinary lives in the community and had known the joys and sorrows of parenthood and family life. The sexual asceticism of the Parfaits was often not based on repression, but on the fact that they had experienced and outlived the sexual urge. Others who entered the priesthood at an early age were not faced with the constant flesh and spirit struggle which St. Augustine describes so graphically and which is inevitable when a youth of average sexual potential turns his thoughts to the Catholic priesthood. The Cathar becoming a Parfait in young manhood was a special kind of individual who, as a Dualist, was capable of recognising and reconciling within himself the impulses of spirit and matter. With him or her it was not a question of repression or even sublimation. The operative fact was that he or she had inherited at birth the capacity for a special type of consciousness which dispensed with the necessity for sexual activity.

Catharism was indeed especially concerned with life at different levels of consciousness. To its exponents this world was Hell because in it we achieved our lowest level of sensitivity. This is what is meant when it is said of the Cathars that to them matter was intrinsically evil. This viewpoint has nothing whatever to do with the special sinfulness of sexuality. Parfaits were indeed tolerant in these matters. This very tolerance has laid them open to the charge of hypocrisy by some Catholic writers. The thinking behind these charges is muddled. Why a Cathar priest should be indicted for tolerance and compassion to sinners when priests of other denominations are exempt from such charges is indeed mysterious. Certainly the Cathars never used sexual morality as a yardstick by which to separate good from evil. Their objection to matter was twofold. Firstly it numbed the perceptions and impeded the capacity to communicate. The human ego, trapped in the flesh, was incapable of such means of psychic communication as clairvoyance, telepathy, and most important of all the gift of healing. This was because the human personality was rivetted in time. It was moulded by

40

regrets for the past and desires for the future. The psyche, on the other hand, was, relative to the ego, emancipated from time. It was in virtue of this emancipation from time that it was capable of what are logically called the psychic gifts of telepathy, precognition and the like. The Parfaits were chosen because of their capacity to function outside the dimensions of chronology. The second reason why the Cathars deplored imprisonment in matter was because of its transitory nature. The Good God made the good spirits and Satan the transient forms. To the Cathars the transitory was to some degree synonymous with what was evil.

One cannot repeat too often that the Cathar attitude to imprisonment in matter can in no sense qualify for the title of puritanical. It is completely unrelated to any question of the sinfulness of sexuality or sensory experience. In many ways it is little different from what we encounter in classical Greek philosophy. We accredit exponents of the latter with a desirable serenity, with a vast and tolerant culture and with the capacity to see life as a whole. When a revered Greek philosopher tells us that the best thing is not to be born we do not immediately describe him as puritanical. We are even a little reluctant to classify him as pessimistic. We afford a respect to Platonists and other Greek philosophers which we do not show to the Cathars. What both mean is simply that, in having to reincarnate, the psyche loses, for the period of its life on this planet, the acute awareness it had in those states of consciousness intervening between our separate lives on earth. This is where Catharism is essentially an optimistic religion. Here we are at our worst but the sun is shining and the leaves are turning with the advent of October. After death, our psyche wholly freed, we will live in a state of greater perception than we have enjoyed on this planet. We will relive all the beauties we have known in this world without being wracked by the agony of their passing.

CHAPTER SIX

It is not until we realise what type of men became Parfaits, and into what a sane and evolutionary world they entered in so doing, that we can understand the significance of the Consolamentum. This was the sole sacrament recognised by the Cathars. It was given under two widely divergent sets of circumstances, firstly to those of mature years and in the full vigour of life who wished to become Parfaits, and secondly to believers at the point of death. In both cases the idea was that the compulsion of the flesh was rejected and the aspirant devoted, or relinquished, himself to the life of the spirit.

One has little more to say of the Consolamentum as administered on the death bed. Attendance of a Parfait at this time was assured by a kind of pact called the Convenanza, through which the croyant arranged to receive the Consolamentum on his death bed and the Parfait undertook to attend him as quickly as possible. There is no doubt that the Consolamentum had immense prestige among the people. It is flattering to human nature to assume that the generality rushed to ensure that they should pass by means of this sacrament through the gateway to the spirit. The fact that so many postponed this privilege till their deathbed leads one to believe that a good number saw it as a more efficient way to heaven than anything offered by the Catholics.

To receive the Consolamentum in the prime of life was a different matter. Technically the recipient abjured the flesh, undertook to live chastely and to follow the prescribed fasts. The latter were far less rigorous than has been supposed. Some of the testimonies made to the Inquisitors by ordinary believers were hearsay evidence of the wildest nature. Nevertheless, though the asceticism of the Cathars has been exaggerated, there has been for centuries an air of mystery about

42

the Consolamentum. It sounds awesome and even frightening. In the prime of life men died to the flesh. To modern ears there is a depressing air of finality about it all. Of course there were compensations. Some have supposed that the Consolamentum conferred on those who received it an insensibility to pain such as that achieved by Yogis walking on coals. This endowed the recipient with the useful asset of being able to resist persecution. Certainly the ritual states clearly that those accepting the Consolamentum must resist all forms of torture applied to them. Sentimental supporters of Catharism have accepted that such an immunity to agony was conferred on the Parfaits through the Consolamentum. It is certainly to be noted that the Catholic historians have recalled how the Parfaits cast themselves almost willingly into the flames, but 'cast' is poetical licence and the aim of such descriptions is to credit the Cathars with suicidal tendencies and to clarify once and for all their morbid preoccupation with the mortification of the flesh. To me it has always seemed that the view that a single ceremony could confer on the recipient such immunity from pain was quite untenable and smacked too much of sentimentality and a lack of critical faculty.

The Consolamentum has come down to us in two forms, the Rituel de Lyon, written in Langue d'Oc and existing in manuscript in the Palais des Arts at Lyon. The other, the Rituel de Florence is in Latin. The former has been translated into French by René Nelli whose translation can be studied with profit. He gives details of the ceremony itself, of the clean table set with a white cloth, the washing of the hands and the touching of the head of the aspirant with a copy of the Gospel according to St. John. In the case of women the officiating priest touched the elbow. The ceremony was performed by a senior member of the Cathar community holding the rank of either bishop or deacon. At its termination a kiss of peace was exchanged between members of the same sex present in the audience.

What may strike the reader on first reading the ritual of Lyons is that there is no startling and openly expressed theological difference between it and the more orthodox rituals of

43

Christianity, be they Roman or Anglican. How could there be? Cathar, Roman, Anglican and Protestant liturgy all derive from the same limited number of scriptural sources. They are all based chiefly on the four Gospels, the Acts and, to a lesser extent, the other books of the New Testament. Stemming as they do from common sources one could not expect any dramatic difference of expression. It is all a matter of interpretation. We have enough evidence from our brief summation of the basic principles of Catharism to see to what degree differences of interpretation can produce a totally different religion from that conceived of by orthodoxy. Another graphic example may emphasise this point. In the Gospel according to St. John we have the phrase, 'By Him were all things made and without Him was nothing made.' The Cathar interpretation of this phrase is totally different from that of orthodox Christian theology. To the orthodox the phrase quoted means that God made everything. To the Cathar its significance is totally different. 'Without Him was nothing made,' meant that the Nothing, the Void, the evil which is the absence of good, was made without God's co-operation, that is by Satan. God was purely love and was only responsible for what was good.

It is therefore possible to read what is left to us of Cathar ritual without finding any crucial difference from the liturgy of orthodoxy. But certain phrases do stand out in the Lyons ritual. First of all, there is the enormous emphasis on self purification. Those who wrote this ritual were greatly concerned with the manner of man aspiring to be a priest. The aspirant is not confronted with thirty-nine articles to which he must subscribe before admission. What the elders are more concerned with is his state of mind and heart. They were always asking, what kind of man is this who wishes to be a Parfait? What will he transmit to others when he lays his hands on them to receive them into the Church? The Catholic Church has always insisted that the sacrament is valid and efficacious independent of the nature of the man who administers it. This is the direct opposite of what was believed by the Cathars. With them it was always the state of purity, the level of being which one had achieved, which determined one's election as a priest.

Secondly, there is in the ritual a special reference to imprisonment in matter. The following passage is pretty unmistakeable. 'Do not have pity on the flesh born of corruption. But have pity on the spirit put in prison.' This passage contains the essence of Catharism in a sentence. After the Council of Constantinople in the eighth century the Roman Church denied the existence of an individual spirit. Man consisted of a body and a soul. He could only aspire to the Spirit by the grace of God through the intermediary of the priesthood and by means of the Catholic sacraments. To the Cathar the soul was a constant and perpetually active channel of communication between the human ego and the spirit. The plane of the soul was that on which the battle between good and evil was fought. When the battle was won in the name of good the Spirit in man was released. Put simply, the purification of the soul to the Catholic was the end of the journey. To the Cathar it was only a half-way house. The Cathar recognised the retarding influence of the body on the soul and how it impeded the latter's ascension to the level of the Spirit. The Catholics did not see life in this way. For them there was a natural world with natural appetites. There was also a supernatural world where, in one kangaroo-like leap, we would be rid of all our appetites and other inconvenient impedimenta. Neither nature nor any kind of evolution, spiritual or otherwise, moves in these uneven bounds. Catharism is far better adapted to the requirements of logic and science.

It must be understood that the Consolamentum was only a primary initiation. It indicated that the Parfait was capable of further training. The aim of the ritual was to increase in a controlled fashion the psychic power of the individual. This was undertaken in most cases to facilitate the capacity to heal. (Natural healing occurs out of chronological time and is essentially an extra-sensory phenomena.) It was the aim of meditation not merely to increase the capacity to canalise the force of goodness in the laying on of hands. In addition the healer was so trained as to be able to project himself in his psychic body to the bedside of the sufferer. Another of the aims of this secondary course in meditation was to enhance the perceptive powers of the individual to enable him to read aright the Dualist symbols presented to him in visions. The most subtle use of the practice of meditation was to increase the perception of the Parfaits specialising in the study of philosophy. This may seem strange to modern eyes for whom philosophy is essentially an intellectual process. That this is so may well be the reason for the low quality of a good deal of what is produced. To the Cathars philosophy was essentially a transcendental experience of revealed truth. It was something we acquire through the last refinements of perception. Philosophic truth was revealed to the mind as a landscape is seen by the eyes. To the Cathars poetic vision was not an imaginative experience or a flight of fancy. It was an insight more intense, more real, more utterly truthful than intuition. It was a piercing into the very nature of truth and it was for this reason that an élite among the Parfaits were especially trained.

The Cathar interest in meditation ties up not only with oriental philosophy as established throughout the ages but also with its modern western adaptation, though too often the latter is obsessionally preoccupied with the teaching of gurus who simply adapt old precepts to the self-indulgence and the get-peace-quick obsessions of their western disciples. There is one factor which distinguishes Cathar practice finally and absolutely from modern techniques. I am not referring to the higher quality and education of the selected Parfaits who instructed their disciples in the caves of the Ariège and elsewhere. In the thirteenth century Languedoc meditation was practised only by the Parfaits. It was realised that the widespread use of meditation among those not ready for it was dangerous. When the mind is emptied too precipitately, in those not mature enough for the experience, it is invaded by lower entities. This is what is meant by Christ's reference to the place swept clean for the seven devils to enter. Cathar meditation was chosen with meticulousness to fit the requirements of each individual. The modern practice of group meditation would have filled them, and rightly, with horror. The number of Parfaits chosen to meditate to the depth that the deeper philosophic truths were revealed was merely a handful. Once again the distinction between those existing at different levels of consciousness was carefully maintained. There was no easygoing assumption, as is encountered in the desperate pseudo-enlightenment of decaying democracy, that given a chance everybody can heal and everybody can see into the secrets of nature. Even among the highly cultured élite of the Parfaits the number trained to examine the ultimate truths was minimal.

What were these mysteries and secret truths revealed to selected Parfaits? This question is the subject of a good deal of semi-mystical speculation, a good deal of which is unfounded. Here Catharism becomes, to its detriment, inextricably mingled with the Graal legend. This is not to say that there are not affinities between the two but that the cup from which Christ drank at the last supper should have found its way to Montségur is beyond the realm of possibility. There were certain symbols revealed to the Parfaits in the process of meditation but the sight of these so-called symbols has been common down the centuries to all Dualist initiates who have reached a certain level of evolution. Nor can all these visionary experiences be regarded merely as symbols. They are real and unvarying materialisations common to people of certain types through three or four millennia, to be considered more as a living alphabet of Dualism than as mere symbols, or, if you will, as something more real and of earlier origin than Jung's archetypal images. The latter are often only a memory of an earlier and more valid experience obscured by the intellectualist interpretations of centuries.

What the inner core of meditative Parfaits were concerned with was the processes involved in the creation of the material world and in the origin of life in its waters and on its surface. They were preoccupied also with the nature of the forces of good and evil and how even these seemingly primary energies are in fact secondary manifestations. It will interest those for whom Catharism was a puritanical religion to know that in the last analysis the basic truths of life were aesthetic, that beauty, that is to say the emanation of an invisible harmony, was more primordial than goodness and evil, and that the latter were fission products of a lost harmony.

I have often heard it said that Dualists are too concerned with good and evil and that the aim of life is to be beyond such conflicting opposites. This is a complete misreading of Dualist philosophy and derives often from a half-knowledge of popularised oriental philosophy. From many points of view it is desirable that we should be beyond good and evil but in this world such a feat is beyond the reach of our psychological antennae. This world is essentially a battleground of good and evil. It is simply useless to assert that evil has no reality when it is responsible for so much disease, both psychiatric and physical. The Cathars believed, as much as the oriental philophers who provided the bedrock of Hinduism and Buddhism, in the necessity of ultimately transcending the world of irreconcilable opposites. They had, however, the good sense to realise that it cannot be achieved in this world except by an especially gifted handful and that this desirable consummation must, for the majority, be relegated to those higher states of consciousness which exist only after what we call death.

This confusion arises from a sloppy and completely inaccurate use of the word dualist. The latter, spelt with a small d, is now used to imply any pair of seemingly immiscible opposites like goodness and evil, and beauty and ugliness. Dualism, with a capital D, is a philosophy whose clean-cut basic principles we have already adequately defined. It accepts, like many other reputable philosophies, the necessity for the merging of opposites. It merely indicates that the latter cannot be achieved by sentimentality, unfounded hope, a smattering of verbal concepts and an inability to face life squarely.

Was there any other special capacity achieved by the training undergone by the Parfaits *after* their reception of the Consolamentum? To answer this question I must revert to our previous statement that the Parfaits were recruited from those with psychic gifts and marked emanatory capacity. After the reception of the Consolamentum the whole aim of the meditation and philosophical studies to which the Parfaits were devoted was to transform themselves from the psychic to the spiritual plane. This was only achieved in the case of a proportion of the Parfaits. The assessment of the tasks which they had to perform was made according to the degree to which this psychological alchemy was achieved. The Cathars believed that, in addition to the body – mind complex we call the human personality, man had a soul and an individualised spirit. They recognised that the possession of psychic gifts, however remarkable, was not an end in itself. How could this be seeing that the psyche was only the vibrating channel by which the human personality communicated with the individualised spirit? In this life we are so often exhorted, often by a cautious and apologetic priesthood, sometimes by an incautious and uninspired laity, not to allow ourselves to become bogged down in the psychic because to do so retards one's spiritual development. All this is well enough in its way but it has to be accepted that for many the way to the spiritual is through the psychic. The longer I live the more I believe the psychic is a stage one must inevitably traverse and that the precipitious leap from the plane of every-day existence to the spiritual is more than flesh and blood can support. It produces a disquieting number of spiritual athletes, many of whom are only obsessional neurotics in disguise.

We have to look at this business of psychic and spiritual levels in terms of communication. At the time of his reception of the Consolamentum the average Parfait was able to communicate by clairvoyance, telepathy and allied gifts. In virtue of his particular level of communication he was especially able to heal the sick. What he developed afterwards was the capacity to give to others something of his essential, inner self, that is to say of his individualised spirit. This distinction between psychic and spiritual activity is exemplified in that miracle of Christ in which he perceived that virtue had gone out of Him. It was His capacity to give of his real self which explains the question we posed previously as to how it was possible for Cathars to die peacefully in the flames without appearing to suffer. So far as the Parfait himself was concerned there were here two processes at work. Withdrawn into the utterly limitless life of the spirit, infinitely more emancipated from time and space than when existing at the level of the psyche, he was immune to

49

earthly pains. This capacity to live in this life at the level of the individualised spirit carried with it the gift of moving into his etheric body and in so doing to escape the pains of this world. (One of the essential differences between psychic and truly spiritual healing is that, when out of the body experiences are involved, the psychic individual is often unaware that he has made his therapeutic journey which occurs without the connivance of his will. The truly spiritual healer* can of his own volition move in and out of his etheric body.)

We have also to consider those to whom the Parfaits administered the Consolamentum before they were doomed to die as heretics. This happened often. The most celebrated occasion was when Bertrand Marty and other Parfaits gave the sacrament to those heretics at Montségur who had refused to abjure and were due to die the next morning. In these circumstances the Parfaits were able to build something of their essential selves into their flock doomed to be sacrificed. This is all contrary to the laws of contemporary psychiatry but the latter has put itself out of court as an interpreter of human behaviour because, except for Jung, it has limited itself to what happens within the frontiers of personality and on the herd plane where the human egos live in competition with each other. By clairvoyance, telepathy and the gift of healing the Parfaits were able to communicate with their flock at the level of the spirit and, through the Consolamentum, they were enabled not merely to communicate at a deep level but to confer on others, for a time at any rate, their own capacity to slip into a timeless sphere beyond the reach of human agony. There can be no doubt that this capacity was transferable by the experienced Parfait to those committed to his charge. This power was only exercised at times of crisis, especially when death at the stake was imminent.

We are right to believe that the Consolamentum by which the ordinand was received in the Church as a Parfait had no

* Spiritual healing in this sense has nothing in common with the contemporary usage of the term. The latter is often vaguely applied to a variety of activities which vary according to the aims and intentions of the sect or group which pursue them. By spiritual healing I mean that achieved at the level of the spirit by the individualised spirit in man.

such tremendous potentialities. It was the prolonged and skilled training which he received afterwards which enabled him to use, through this sacrament, his own immense potentialities for the benefit of others when the hour was crucial. Looked at in this light the statement made in the Consolamentum that the recipient is required to resist torture by fire and water is highly relevant and abundantly justified. This was one of the rarer but specific purposes of the Consolamentum. It accounts for the serenity and indeed joy with which the victims met their fate and which Catholic observers record so reluctantly for us. The discarnate sources which have broken the silence of seven centuries have emphasised the unique nature of what in the last extremity could be communicated by way of the Consolamentum. Some of what I have been told to add about the Consolamentum and the training of the Parfaits has been obtained from discarnate sources. It is absolutely essential that what they say should be admitted as evidence. To exclude it would be to deny the existence of truth by revelation. It can be said that to accept blindly as truth what is obtained from discarnate sources is to commit one of the oldest possible errors known to man. But when discarnate sources have revealed themselves as capable of giving meticulous advice expressed in numbers and verified by the canons of history and science one must surely credit them with accuracy and veracity. Those who have read some of my other works will realise that, in directing me to the Montserver family. Braïda, dead seven centuries, dictated on more than one occasion the numerals 609 on different pieces of paper. This was found later to represent the number on the folio in the archives of Toulouse which contained the most comprehensive references to the Montserver family. Such undeviating clarity has characterised all my contacts with those who, alive in the thirteenth century, have shown the capacity to communicate with us.

In inquiring into the admissibility of truth by revelation I am only following a Platonic tradition which is of greater scope and of more tested value than the myopic self-sterilising attitude which insists that truth is something which can only be arrived at in a laboratory. In any case what I have to say in this book is overwhelmingly based on historical sources. Above all it should be remembered that my knowledge of Catharism is derived from the meticulous sifting of evidence necessitated by my earlier books on this subject. It was only after I had served my apprenticeship verifying, according to the exacting requirements of science and history, what had been said to me by Mrs. Smith, the central figure of *The Cathars and Reincarnation*, and by Miss Mills, who played a similar role in *We Are One Another*, that I moved into closer contact with the discarnates and had more communication with them.

CHAPTER SEVEN

In the first years of the thirteenth century the heresy continued to expand and the Papacy became increasingly disquieted. Pope Innocent III sent papal legates to the Languedoc, and particularly to the Count of Toulouse, to insist that he did his utmost to extirpate the Cathars. Raymond VI was favourably inclined towards the heresy but never came out openly as its champion. He was a charming, enlightened, vacillating and unheroic character who played a cat and mouse game with the Papacy according to the degree of pressure put on him. He was excommunicated on more than one occasion. It is said in his defence that it was necessary for him to trim his sails in order to keep his kingdom but his policy failed absolutely. He could not have done worse had he maintained a steadfast opposition to the wishes of the Papacy.

In 1204 Pope Innocent III sent the Abbé of Citeaux to direct his papal legates, Pierre de Castelnau and Raoul de Fontfroide, to intensify the measures to be taken against the heretics. He also approached the French king Phillipe Auguste, to seek his support in a purifying operation. The latter sidestepped the suggestion.

A further and determined attempt was made in 1206 to undermine the strength of the heresy. Dominic de Guzman, a Spanish monk, set out with a companion to undertake a preaching mission. This differed from its predecessors in being unaccompanied by any evidence of luxury, pomp and circumstance. Dominic and his modest entourage dressed austerely and lived sparsely. In point of fact they emulated the habits of the Bonshommes, thereby establishing a tradition which endures to this day. The Dominican Order has always been the first in the Catholic Church to seize on the virtues of its antagonists and to modify them to its own uses.

53

When psychoanalytic theory swept like a plague over Europe it was anathematised by the Vatican. When, however, it was evident that Freudian analysis had come to stay, the Church reversed its policy and priests were excellently trained in analytical methods. Once again it was the Dominicans who undertook to fashion the tools of the enemy to their own use.

Dominic embarked on what was essentially a preaching mission to bring back the lost sheep to the fold by persuasion and argument but made no bones about the fact that if persuasion were inadequate force would follow. He said unequivocally that if words failed the sword would follow. His efforts attracted a good deal of derision from the bystanders and made few converts. He succeeded in founding a convent at Prouille for girls who had defected from Catharism. This structure was not exactly congested. Apart from this he made little headway.

It is a tribute to the tolerance of the Languedoc that during this period there was a celebrated encounter between Dominic and the Cathar Bishop Guilhabert de Castres at Fanjeaux. It was agreed that Catholics and Cathars should dispute the truth of their separate interpretations of the Scriptures. Presumably the two above-mentioned celebrities were captains of their respective teams. For what happened next we are indebted to Catholic sources. It was agreed that each champion should throw into the flames his particular version of the Scriptures. Whichever remained unconsumed was the true gospel. The Cathar version was placed in the fire and promptly consumed. (What, incidentally, was the Cathar version of the Scriptures? It can only have been what was in common use throughout Christendom. The Rituel de Lyon is liturgical and not scriptural). It is inevitable that the Cathar copy is reported to have burnt freely. The script in the possession of the Catholics not only eluded the flames but bounded up and struck the roof with a resounding crack. A piece of the roof timber is preserved to this day in the garden at Fanjeaux of the house where the encounter took place. It is slightly stained over a part of its surface. That this was ever caused by fire is possible but doubtful.

St. Dominic achieved other miracles, in one of which ears of corn in the neighbourhood of Montreal and Fanjeaux were turned to blood. This was indeed most appropriate. In modern phraseology it could be described as precognitive. The whole neighbourhood was soon to be drenched in blood.

The antipathy shown by the populace to the Catholic preachers continued. Dominic, it seemed, had come too late. The Languedoc remained obstinately addicted to Catharism. Nevertheless it is strange that in these seemingly favourable years the Cathar bishop, Guilhabert de Castres, approached Raymond de Perella to persuade him to rebuild the Château of Montségur, the ruins of which were perched at the top of a mountain in the Ariège. Montségur was later to become the ultimate refuge of Catharism. Was Guilhabert clairvoyant and did he see, in the midst of this period of fair weather, the approaching tempest and the ruin it would cause?

The Pope's opportunity came with the murder of one of his legates, Pierre de Castelnau. It is said, without evidence, that the crime was committed by a young knight acting at the instigation of Raymond of Toulouse. The Pope addressed himself to Philippe Auguste of France, asking for his co-operation in raising a crusade against the Albigeois. The king was preoccupied with the menace from England and elsewhere and extracted himself adroitly from the responsibility. He nevertheless collaborated in the recruitment of an army which descended on the Languedoc by way of the Rhone valley. This force was raised essentially by great nobles from what is now north and central France, from Flanders and from the German provinces, with one or two enthusiastic strays from England.

Before mentioning the main features of this war it might perhaps be instructive to outline the conditions of service. The Pope granted to those taking part in it complete remission of all sins, not only those committed in the past but any which might occur in the future. It is doubtful if any army in history has ever provided such attractive conditions of service. One can well understand that the recruited host equalled the immense proportions attributed to it by its main chroniclers. Among other benefits was the cancelling of all debts contracted to Jewish money lenders.

One point should be noticed. This was the only time in

history that the word crusade was used to describe an army fighting against Europeans and Christians. The term had previously only been employed against Asiatics and non-Christians. Certainly the Crusaders had killed many Christians on the way to the Holy Land but this was only a side issue and committed from no worse motives than the impulse to kill and plunder.

The Crusade began initially as a practical demonstration of the Church militant. It was commanded by Arnaud-Amaury, the Abbé of Citeaux. He was accompanied by members of the higher French nobility, such as the Duke of Burgundy and the Count of Nevers. Catholic apologists have said that force was not applied to the Albigeois until all efforts at persuasion had failed. They do not explain why, when the force was exercised, it was directed and manipulated by the Church of Christ. It was under the direction of the Abbé that the crusaders achieved one of their most dramatic successes.

The Crusade got off to a good start at Béziers. Roger Trencavel III, Viscount of Carcassonne and Béziers, was a young man in his twenties. He visited Béziers before it was invested, regarded it as capable of defending itself and went post haste to Carcassonne to arrange for its defence because he realised it was bound to be attacked. Béziers fell, due to the fact that an intemperate attack on the part of the besieged gave entry to the investing army. What followed was horrific even by the high standards of the Middle Ages. Some chroniclers say that all the inhabitants of the city were massacred. Some put the number at thirty thousand. It is said that six or seven thousand were massacred in the church of St. Madeleine where they had taken refuge. The victims were Catholic as well as Cathar. It is probable that the Catholic victims outnumbered the Cathars seeing that they had taken refuge in a Catholic church. It is a great pity that we have no reliable records of the population of Béziers. One can only point out that it was one of the great cities of the prosperous and, for those days, highly populated Languedoc.

What stands out with certainty about the massacre on July 22nd, 1209 is its appalling extent and its indiscriminate nature. It is recorded that when one of the Catholic knights wished to know whom to kill, in itself a curious question, the Church militant in the person of the Abbé of Cîteaux replied, 'Kill them all. God will know his own.'

It is remarkable how, until recent times, there has been little comment on this horror. Since the great increase of interest in Catharism in the last three decades there have been attempts on the part of faithful Catholics to minimise this outrage. It may be true that the number of casualties has been exaggerated by some writers. This applies to any battle or siege since the world began. What is beyond doubt is that, when it occurred, this was possibly the most appalling massacre Europe had seen for centuries. Its magnitude has been conveniently forgotten.

A more arguable defence of the Catholic apologists is that the Crusaders themselves were not responsible and that their paid mercenaries, called routiers, got out of hand. This argument is ironical in that the employment of routiers was one of the grievances of the Papacy against the Counts of Toulouse and other nobles in the Languedoc and its vicinity. Even if the defence offered by these Catholic apologists is admissable, why should the Crusaders themselves have employed bands which had been officially anathematized by the Papacy in the latter half of the twelfth century? These particular factors are unimportant compared with the responsibility of Innocent III. In forgiving in advance the sins of all those who took part in the Crusade, he was inviting atrocities from a body of men with promising qualifications in the practice of their profession. One need not linger on the lesser crime of exercising the power of the Church in a temporal and military fashion involving the shedding of blood. There was already a precedent for this in the previous expedition of 1167 which had also been led by a priest.

The effect of the sack of Béziers was stunning. It was somewhat analogous to the effects of atomic bombing in the second world war. It was a horror of a magnitude exceeding anything in the memory of the people of the Midi. A considerable number of the minor nobility abandoned any resistance and made their submission to the invading forces.

After Béziers, Carcassonne. The latter was the greatest fortress of its day. It could justifiably have been regarded as a prize which could only fall after months or years of siege. It succumbed in less than a month after the sack of Béziers. That year was a dry summer. The water supply of the fortress failed. There was an outbreak, among the garrison and in the city, of what could have been either dysentery or typhoid. The young commander, Roger Trencavel, was advised by his kinsman Pierre II, Catholic king of Aragon, to treat with the enemy. Trencavel unfortunately accepted this advice which was almost certainly given in good faith. The King of Aragon had no special wish to see the Northern lords, advance guards of the kingdom of France, installed so near his territory. Trencavel himself did not take the initiative in the matter. He was offered, by the investing crusaders, a safe-conduct to discuss terms. Once arrived at the enemies' camp he was taken into custody.

Deprived of their leader, the capacity for resistance of the Carcassonnais was diminished. An entry was effected but when the occupying troops entered the town a large proportion of the inhabitants had already left the city. This circumstance prevented a repetition of the massacre at Béziers. Trencavel was subsequently incarcerated in a tower of his own fortress. He died shortly afterwards. Opinion is divided as to whether he died of the prevailing malady or whether he was poisoned by the orders of the enemy, now commanded by de Montfort. The shameful episode of this breach of faith on the part of the besiegers was all to be foreseen, as were the other atrocities, in the Papal clause which forgave sins in advance.

There can be no doubt whatever that what happened in the first month of the Crusade was a crushing blow to Catharism and to the civilisation and integrity of the Languedoc. In actual fact the wars, with periods of intermission, were to continue another forty-six years until the fall, or surrender, of Queribus in 1255. But, though the Languedoc fought back, it never really recovered from this appalling start. The outrageous massacre at Béziers showed the inhabitants what they had to expect from the invading forces. The rapid fall of the supposedly invincible Carcassonne had a crushing effect on the morale of the population. Also the nature of the civilisation of the Languedoc contributed to its own downfall. In that country the feudal system was already breaking down and being replaced by a more open social structure in which the representatives of commerce played a more important rôle than elsewhere. Had the Languedoc been less advanced sociologically it might have put up a better fight. Toulouse resembled to some extent a North Italian city state. But city states tend to go their own way independent of the threat to their neighbours. This is in fact what happened in the Midi. Trencavel of Carcassonne and the house of Toulouse were on bad terms and made no attempt to collaborate with each other. Raymond VI of Toulouse was indeed with the investing Catholic army. This was one of the humiliating penances imposed on him. Seen across seven and a half centuries it is a marvel how this enigmatic character retained the affection of his subjects. One moment he was offering up heretics as sacrifices to placate the Papacy, the next he was tolerating them and availing himself of their services. No doubt all this was based on the customary alibi supplied by the historians that it was necessary for him to act in this equivocal manner in order to maintain the integrity of his kingdom. (This is an argument which above all supports the Cathar idea that all earthly hierarchies are essentially evil.) Even if this attitude were ethically justifiable it remains a fascinating source of speculation why this dynasty retained the affection and loyalty of its subjects. Perhaps it was a matter of personal charm. What is more likely is that the house of Toulouse offered to the common people a freedom, a standard of living and a degree of civilisation they could not find elsewhere.

After the fall of Carcassonne the true nature of the great Crusade became evident. Pope Innocent III desired nothing more nor less than the complete extirpation of heresy from the Languedoc. To this end he aimed at the removal from power of those nobles who had been notorious protectors of heretics. After the fall of Carcassonne he desired to transfer to other hands the territories of the defeated Viscount. Carcassonne and Béziers were offered in turn to the Duke of Burgundy and the Counts of Nevers and St. Pol. All three refused. It is impossible to say whether they wished to avoid the responsibility or if they had genuine scruples. A contemporary witness, Guillaume de

Tudèle, part aurthor of the *Chanson de la Croisade*, credits them with the highest motives. We can afford to give them the benefit of the doubt, if only to lighten a story which is almost undeviatingly sordid.

After the refusal of the higher aristocracy to consider his tainted wares Innocent III hawked round the fief of Carcassonne and Béziers among the minor nobility. The choice of his commission fell on Simon de Montfort. He could not have picked a better man. De Montfort combined in his person all the brutish religiosity, avarice, and aggression which made him not only an ideal hammer of heretics but the perfect instrument for the consolidation of stolen territories.

It was in virtue of his office of Vicomte of Carcassonne and Béziers that de Montfort became leader of the crusaders. One of the conditions of recruitment had been that the nobility need only serve forty days. At the expiration of this period the invading host disintegrated to a considerable degree. The Count of Nevers was among the first to leave. He was closely followed by the Duke of Burgundy. This was perhaps just as well. The tension between them was such that even the contemporary Catholic historian, Pierre de Vaulx Cernay, remarked that each day observers feared that these two gentlemen would kill each other. Their previous sins pardoned by forty days' service, the higher aristocracy left the Languedoc and took their men with them. De Montfort was left to consolidate his gains with a small band of knights and a greatly reduced army.

The war now under way had ceased to be a direct battle between the Languedoc and the Papacy over a question of heresy. One cannot in all honesty say that the great lords of the Midi were prepared to die for the protection of the Cathars though in some areas the minor nobility were amazingly devoted. But defence of, and tolerance for, Catharism was one of the features of the civilisation of the Languedoc. This was threatened by a militant Papacy, devoid of scruple and rooted in temporal power. It had to be combated by force of arms. Equally it would be ludicrous to say that the Northern lords were instigated by what we would now call religious motives. Certainly fidelity to orthodox Christianity played an immense role in their desire to take part in the crusade. One cannot doubt their sincerity in this matter. They believed in Heaven and Hell and in the magical efficiency of the Sacraments. It was only natural that they should be horrified by a heresy which denied the efficacy of this treasured prescription for the saving of their souls. The latter were, to them, the continuation of their individuality as they themselves knew it. In this they were average orthodox believers at a time when the Church was at a low ebb. They cannot be blamed if what they believed was unrelated to religious experience. In this particular they were no better or worse than most of their contemporaries. Perhaps they were more ferocious. We cannot even say this with impunity. They had, after all, been absolved in advance.

But, quite apart from all questions of religion, self-aggrandisement and loot became the main motive of the Crusaders. The civilisation of the Midi was richer than their own. Once invested with the supreme command, Simon de Montfort acquired possessions for himself and his confrères and, in so doing, dispossessed their rightful owners. It is probably true to say that some of the French nobles recoiled in disgust from the suggestion that they should seize the possessions of others. There were apparently some who had merely taken part in the Crusade in order to see heresy suppressed. It is too much to assume that all those who left de Montfort had acquired as much loot as they could carry.

CHAPTER EIGHT

The Crusade is inseparably associated with the name of Simon de Montfort. An impressive proportion of English readers assume that this was the same individual who, for better or worse, presented us with one of our earlier sketches of a Parliament. The crusading de Montfort was the father of the man who made what was, on the whole, a civilising impact on our history.

The elder de Montfort was a period piece. Born of the minor nobility of Northern France, he was a brutal, ruthless and determined illiterate who had no doubt whatever that he was a loyal son of the Church and that the massacres and spoilations he initiated were to the glory of God. There cannot be any doubt that he sincerely believed that his own glory was coincidental with that of the Saviour. Heresy was a blow in the face of God and it was the duty of a good Christian to kill heretics. That the teaching of Christ ever came to be the basis of such exuberant bellicosity is a matter for wondering reflection. An intense, and later ferocious, sectarianism had been growing in the Church since the first two centuries after Christ. Julian the Apostate, who lived in the fourth century, saw that Christianity was becoming a dangerous and repressive international theocracy and wished to return to the older cults. De Montfort and his kind were as much conditioned to think and act as they did as are young Communists of today or young Nazis of yesterday. That they did so in the name of Christ is perhaps especially unfortunate.

There is now a considerable literature on the Albigensian wars. It is unfortunate that the majority of it is in French, but then it has always been a baleful habit of foreigners to write in their own language. In the first nine years de Montfort is the key figure. Following his investiture as Vicomte of Carcassonne and Béziers he acquired, without much difficulty, the submission of several towns. Among them were Fanjeaux, Limoux, Montréal and Mirepoix. In the foothills of La Montagne Noire the defenders of Cabaret resisted stubbornly. In 1210 resistance hardened elsewhere. Bram, which lies off the main road from Carcassonne to Montréal, resisted three days. Conscientious to a fault de Montfort seized the garrison of a hundred, blinded and removed the noses and upper lips of all but one of this number, and sent the latter, who was left favoured with one eye, to lead his mutilated companions on a propaganda march to Cabaret.

In the summer of the same year de Montfort laid siege to Minerve, a hill fortress in arid country and one of the strongest bastions to be held by Cathar sympathisers. Famine and thirst necessitated a capitulation. (There must have been something fundamentally lacking in the water supply of the fortresses of the Languedoc. It failed at Carcassonne, Minerve and later at Termes.) There were one hundred and forty Parfaits within the walls of Minerve. In a mood of unusual clemency they were given the opportunity to save their lives by denying their faith. This unreasonable tolerance was disturbing to Robert de Mauvoisin, one of de Montfort's more zealous captains, who asked if it would not be better that they should be dispatched forthwith. The Abbé of Citeaux, no longer in command but still exercising some influence from the wings, reassured this conscientious officer and said that it was extremely unlikely that any Cathar would avail himself of this open-hearted opportunity for salvation. The Abbé proved a reliable prophet. The hundred and forty Cathars were duly burnt. A simple monument records this massacre. Ironically enough it is placed exactly opposite the door of the Catholic church.

Termes was a harder nut to crack. The castle is situated on the top of a hill in the arid and desolate mountains known as the Corbières. It was stubbornly defended by Raymond de Termes, a worthy member of a family devoted to Catharism and which numbered among its main members Benoit de Termes, Cathar Bishop of Razes. The Summer of 1210, a derisive background for the agony of the Languedoc, was hot and dry. Once again the water supply failed. The defenders were forced to negotiate but the night after the capitulation was arranged there was torrential rain. The cisterns were refilled and the defenders resumed the fight next morning. Unfortunately the water in the cisterns was polluted, an epidemic broke out and the garrison were forced to abandon the château.

As the war continued the capture by de Montfort of the strongholds of Catharism was accompanied by increasing barbarism. The reduction of strong points in the Middle Ages was never a humane procedure. What distinguished de Montfort was that, in his brutality, he was so conscientious and devoted to detail. Perhaps he wished to emphasise the moral superiority of the northern races. In the early April of 1211 he laid siege to Lavaur. It was defended by Aimery de Montréal, son of Blanche de Laurac, a Parfaite noted for her piety and kindness, and brother of the chatelaine Guiraude whose charity equalled that of her mother. The town was taken by storm. Aimery de Montréal was rushed to the gibbet with eighty knights who had fought with him. The gibbet collapsed and the victims were slaughtered like cattle. The mass slaughter of the aristocracy was unusual even for the Middle Ages. Dame Guiraude was offered for the amusement of the soldiery. She was then thrown down a well and buried under an avalanche of stones.

Lavaur paid dearly for the charity of its ruling family. The town had attracted a large number of Parfaits and devoted croyants who had come there to escape persecution. Four hundred Cathars were burnt at Lavaur. This was the biggest auto-da-fé of the whole crusade. People with a superficial knowledge of Catharism regard Montségur as the culminating tragedy. So it was, in that it involved the destruction of a great spiritual bastion, but the Parfaits burnt at Montségur were only half the number of those who died at Lavaur.

The tragedy of the Languedoc was that it had no such devoted and implacable leader as de Montfort. The Count of Toulouse, anti-clerical, essentially tolerant and devoted to his pleasures, had adopted a changing policy towards the Catholic invaders. He had started the war ignominiously riding with the invading armies and doing nothing in particular. His career was an intricate pattern of excommunication, avoiding excommunication and alternately placating and defying the Pope. A meeting with the Papal legates in 1211 required that he should cease to protect Jews and heretics. It is interesting that even to be the former was a crime against the Church. Raymond was required to destroy the châteaux and fortresses of his barons and knights who were forbidden to reside in the city of Toulouse. It was even laid down that they should dress in plebian clothing and not eat more than two kinds of meat. The petty viciousness of these religious requirements is, in its way, as revealing as the major horrors committed by the Crusaders. This was too much for Raymond to swallow. Even then he did not have immediate recourse to arms. It is constantly urged in his favour that he wished to spare his people the horror of war. It is certainly possible that this could have been one of his motives. What is certain is that, whatever he intended, he failed completely. In addition, his relations with the other great lords in the south-west were loose and variable. The Languedoc suffered because, within its frontiers, the feudal system was in a state of partial decomposition, and had not been replaced by a spirit of nationalism.

In 1213 there was the first major confrontation between Raymond VI and de Montfort. This occurred at Muret, a few miles to the south of Toulouse. In this battle the Catholic King of Aragon, Pierre II, joined forces with Raymond to repel the northern invaders. It is ironic that Pierre had previously been commended by the Pope for his efforts against the infidel Moors in Spain. Be that as it may, he had no desire to see northern Frenchmen encroaching so closely on his territory. The battle of Muret was an utter catastrophe. It was the graveyard of hope for Catharism and the Languedoc.

On the face of it everything at Muret was in favour of the southern forces. They greatly outnumbered those of de Montfort. They had also the protection of an armed camp. According to the usually accepted version the battle was lost when Pierre of Aragon, in an excess of foolhardiness and ill-conceived chivalry, abandoned the security of the camp for an injudicious assault on de Montfort's forces. It is usually argued that Raymond of Toulouse, now actually engaged in the defence of his own patrimony, tried to dissuade him from so doing. Certainly Raymond's plan to allow de Montfort to attack, to contain him by crossbows and to counter attack later, seems sensible enough. It appears that to the entourage of the King of Aragon it was equivalent to cowardice. The upshot of this difference was that Raymond retired, like Achilles, to his tent. The King of Aragon launched a frontal attack on the enemy and was killed in the process.

The defeat at Muret was crucial. The fall of Montségur has aroused the public imagination more but from the political point of view Muret was of infinitely greater significance. Had the battle been won de Montfort might well have been discredited. So far as troops were concerned he was always living on a shoe string. A united front between the dominions of Aragon and Toulouse could have provided an impenetrable barrier to the Northern hordes. But Raymond VI was not especially gifted in the construction of enduring unions.

After Muret Raymond and his son left Toulouse and took refuge in Provence. Here, in spite of his variable and unheroic record and his unmistakeable failures, he was received with touching loyalty. In the confused war which followed Raymond achieved some successes and ultimately re-established himself in Toulouse. De Montfort attacked it in due course and was killed on June 25th, 1218. His skull was shattered by a stone hurled from a mangonneau, a kind of glorified catapult. Tradition has it that this machine was worked by women. This could well have been so. Women took an active part in the sieges of Fanjeaux and Montréal and later at Montségur.

The devastation caused by de Montfort was immense. It is estimated that four hundred villages and towns disappeared from the map as a result of his depredations. What had been the centre of European civilisation and a thickly populated area degenerated into one of the most depressed and backward communities. It is no exaggeration to say that the Languedoc never recovered from de Montfort. Lequenne, who in 1954 wrote *Le Drame Cathare*, was a judge at Béziers. His first interest in Catharism was determined by his feeling for atmosphere. He felt that the country was still afflicted and denuded by its past history.

De Montfort has been regarded as a faithful son of the Church. This title is thoroughly justified if one considers the Catholic Church in its undeniable role as a temporal power of immense significance. He has also been described as a paladin of law and order who performed a necessary, if at times ruthless, function. This latter view is untenable. He was a pitiless invader and appropriator of other people's goods, in a country not his own and which had proferred no menace to him, his kind, and his sovereign. It is interesting to read what was said of him by the contemporary reporter who wrote the *Chanson de la Croisade* and who was at the beginning a supporter of it. 'If, by killing men and shedding blood, by ruining souls, by facilitating murder, by believing evil counsels, by instigating conflagrations, destroying the nobility, abolishing honour, by making pride victorious, by stimulating evil and extinguishing good, if by killing women and slaughtering infants one can in this world achieve salvation in Christ, he ought to wear a crown and be resplendent in the heavens.'

What does stand out with extraordinary clarity is the faithfulness of the nobility and people of the Languedoc to the Parfaits. In many cases it would have been so easy for a harassed gentry to have disembarrassed themselves of people who were attracting so much trouble on their heads. In the first decade of the wars there was no question of trading heretics in return for either a local or general peace. During these horrifying years the Parfaits continued to preach and to succour the people. They moved constantly from place to place and never lacked shelter even though those who harboured them risked their lives in so doing. It is a tribute to the loyalty of all classes that, though many Parfaits died in the first decade of the war, there were no casualties among the bishops and higher clergy such as Guilhabert de Castres and Bertrand Marty who, throughout this dreadful epoch, never failed to preach the Word and perform their other duties.

CHAPTER NINE

With the disappearance of Simon de Montfort from the scene a wave of optimism swept through the Languedoc and it was as though the country had been delivered from a nightmare. De Montfort was succeeded by his son, Amaury, whose general incompetence was such that the word Maury infiltrated the country speech and to this day signifies stupidity.

Raymond VI of Toulouse died in 1272. This man, in his lifetime the ruler of the richest dominions in Christendom, could not, in death, find a resting place for his body. He died excommunicated. He made an attempt on his death bed to make his peace with the Church but failed to do so and was denied the last Sacraments. It is an extraordinary reflection on the power of the Church that for twenty-five years his son vainly implored that he should be granted Christian burial. His bones were ultimately dispersed but his skull was saved by the intervention of the Hospital of St. John of Jerusalem. Raymond VI goes down to history as a tolerant, good-natured individual, in his outlook centuries ahead of his time but not born to be a hero. He has been painted as a fervent but at times clandestine supporter of Catharism. This is something of an exaggeration. That he admired and tolerated it in the days of peace is indisputable. It is equally evident that he was prepared to detach himself from it in darker times. He never lost the affection and respect of his subjects in spite of his unsuccessful vacillations. It can only be that he represented a standard of tolerance, humanity and comfortable living which they could not find elsewhere.

The new count, Raymond VII was a better leader than his father but a less attractive character. He had nothing like his father's sympathy for the Cathars, and there is no evidence that he ever aspired to be thought any other than an orthodox Catholic. The fact that he was excommunicated more than once is no evidence that he was basically a heretic. This sentence was automatically inflicted on anyone known to give shelter to a heretic. So far as the Roman Church was concerned he came into this category because so many of his subjects, including the nobility, were addicted to Catharism. We have no proof that Raymond VII was not fighting for the Languedoc and his own patrimony rather than for Catharism. Indeed from some points of view his record is contemptible. As a placatory gesture to his Catholic aggressors he burnt eighty Cathars at Moissac and seized, and subsequently burnt, four Cathars from Montségur. This could not have happened in his father's time.

Whatever his faults Raymond VII had, by 1224, succeeded in freeing the Languedoc from the invaders. The peace which followed was illusory. By 1226 the Crusaders were on the march again. Though nothing could exceed the dramatic horror of the first years of the Crusade the situation at this time was potentially worse for the Languedoc. The crown of France was now fully committed to the conquest of the Midi. Louis VIII acted where his more circumspect father had hesitated. France and the papacy were now officially identified in a war of aggression. Raymond VII of Toulouse, who had tried hard to accommodate the papacy was excommunicated in his absence. The same sentence was passed, under similar conditions, on the Counts of Foix and Béziers.

The war which followed repeated the horrors of 1209. Marmande was a small scale Béziers. Five thousand people were slaughtered. Guillaume de Tudele gives a horrific description of men, women and children being hacked to pieces. Marmande, and the devastation of other towns and villages, had the required propaganda effect. Towns like Carcassonne, Béziers, Arles and Orange hastened to make peace with the invaders. At this juncture the relatively independent constitution of the councils of these places was a disadvantage. The people had more say than elsewhere in the government of their cities and the people had had enough. Avignon resisted stoutly, but then it had not known the horrors afflicting the country further west. At this stage Raymond VII had little support other than that of the Count of Foix and the younger Trencavel of Carcassonne and Béziers, son of the man who had died a prisoner in his own castle in the former city.

Louis VIII of France died in 1226. His widow, Blanche of Castille, directed the war with unremitting ferocity. In 1227 the region of the Tarn and the environs of Toulouse were ravaged. Unable to achieve crushing victories in battle the royal troops embarked on a policy of systematic devastation of farms, vineyards, wheatfields and orchards.

With the Languedoc exhausted by years of ferocious warfare and the threat of famine, Raymond VII concluded, in 1229 at Meaux, an ignominious peace. By its terms the French were granted a firm foothold in the Languedoc and it was clearly accepted that Raymond of Toulouse, along with such nobles as the Counts of Foix and Béziers, were vassals of the King of France. The walls of Toulouse were in part demolished. Raymond even agreed to do public penance and to be whipped before the altar of Notre Dame in Paris. One can only assume that such an humiliating contract was necessitated by the total devastation of the Languedoc. It is interesting that, like his father, Raymond VII never lost face with his people.

After the peace of 1229 the story of the Languedoc centres round the efforts of the Catholic Church, supported by the French, to cleanse it completely from the contamination of heresy. In spite of almost insanely vindictive legislation these efforts largely failed. Catharism continued to be actively practised. We have records of those attending reunions presided over by such eminent Cathars as Guilhabert de Castres. The nobility sheltered the Cathars and led sporadic raids against the French invaders and the exacting clergy. Resistance was particularly fierce in the city of Toulouse. The Count did little to stop it. If he was not personally attracted to Catharism he was certainly infuriated by the tyranny of the Church.

The persecution of the Cathars was intensified with the formation of the Inquisition in 1233. Nothing of the nature of this organisation had ever appeared before in history. There had previously been an unofficial and loosely organised inquisition of bishops and Vatican nominees who had examined and punished deviations from the faith, but it was not until the formation of the Holy Office that the world was presented with the spectacle of an organisation prepared to kill, starve and dispossess those who had deviated a hair's breadth from its own theological preoccupations. No other major religion has ever produced such an organisation. There are secular organisations which have acted with equal ferocity and efficiency but, unlike the Inquisition, they did not last for seven centuries. Under its domination the blessings of peace in the Languedoc were as insupportable and nauseating as the horrors of war. In these agonising years there were frequent mass burnings of heretics. Two hundred and ten perished at Moissac. Before 1233 the persecution of heretics had been inhuman and nauseating but less organised. The courts designed to try heretics acted often with appalling severity but some of the bishops were more clement than others. The earlier courts were directed against individual heretics but did not aim at producing a theological climate in which heresy would be impossible. It was only with the establishment of the Inquisition that this became possible.

The Inquisition was recruited from the Dominicans. Though Dominic had little to show for his proselytizing in the Midi he was gifted, or cursed, with an energy and a degree of devotion and austerity notably absent in other religious orders and among the parochial clergy of the Midi. Dominic's achievement was to mechanise the impulse to persecute and to establish a watertight system of juridical illegality which was to do admirable service for centuries, though it is doubtful if, after the beginning of the fourteenth century, it maintained the degree of efficiency it had shown in the first hundred years after its inception. It was at its competent best in dealing with the Albigeois and the Templars.

The punishment for being a heretic and persisting in one's faith was death by burning. This meant that no Parfait or ordinary believer who persisted in his beliefs could escape the stake. This is simply undeniable and does not merit discussion.

If a heretic abjured his faith under interrogation he was not necessarily burnt at the stake but was punished in one of the ways enumerated below. If, however, having once abjured the faith he relapsed again, he was automatically burnt. This often happened. It was common for ordinary croyants to deny their faith under torture and interrogation. Sometimes when these methods ceased to be applied they reaffirmed their Cathar beliefs and were duly burnt. It is interesting to reflect on the number of Parfaits, as distinct from ordinary croyants, who abandoned the faith during the years of persecution from 1209 onwards. Three is the maximum number possible according to the records. Only one abjured under interrogation.

All the possessions of a person convicted of, and persisting in, heresy, were forfeited. In the case of a noble all those subservient to him were released from all vassalage and from all contractual obligations made to him.

Where an individual did not appear to answer a charge levelled against him by the Inquisition he was assumed guilty and the appropriate sentence passed in his absence.

There was an imposing list of punishments for those convicted of heresy and subsequently recanting, and for contact with heresy. These included imprisonment for life or for years, confiscation of property, obligation to go on pilgrimage, sometimes to the Holy Land and often for years, and corporal punishment. Heretics were often condemned to wear a yellow cross, the dimensions of which were carefully stipulated, sewn on to the garments of the victim. The Nazis adopted an identical measure against the Jews. Plus ça change, plus c'est la même chose. This particular infliction meant something more than public infamy. It involved the removal from the victim of all prospects of employment and all means of sustenance. Anybody endeavouring to help him by giving him food or shelter came under the edict of the Inquisition and was liable to the same punishments ordered for heresy itself. Nobles were declared outlaws and to have forfeited their possessions and the rights which went with them. These dispossessed nobility were known as *faidits*. They took to the maquis and continued for years as focal points of resistance against the northern invaders.

Ferocious as may seem the sentences against confessed and proven heretics they provide us with only a minor view of the picture. The major activity of the Inquisition was directed else-where. Its great virtue was that it saw early what was its main target, that is to say the concealers and protectors of heresy. Here again it was not difficult to discover the names of those who, in the numerous châteaux in the Languedoc, had enter-tained and provided shelter for the Cathars. The nobility in the Languedoc and the Corbières were so solidly Cathar that the Inquisition had no real need for spies and informers. Their aim, however, was not merely to punish all those who had had the most passing contact with the Cathars but to create an atmo-sphere of terror so intense that no Cathar would know where to lay his head with safety in the Midi or to know where his next meal came from.

It was enough to have been seen in the company of a heretic to be convicted and punished according to one or other of the set forms. To have attended a Cathar meeting, to have 'adored' a Parfait, that is to say to have made one of the prescribed genu-flections, was inescapable evidence of guilt. Even to have been in the company of Cathars, unknowingly and in childhood, was regarded as indictable. To have called in a doctor with Cathar affiliations was a heinous crime because one had knowingly and willingly made contact with a heretic. To have shared a meal in a house with company one did not know to be Cathar was also punishable.

The interrogations pursued by the Inquisition were at many times and in many areas less concerned with the punishment of the malefactors presented than with the unravelling of infor-mation about the whole Cathar network. In this they resembled the Gestapo. The latter organisation was, however, not only more tolerant but its scope was less and it was less efficient. It was not concerned with those the accused had met forty or fifty years before as a child. We have no evidence that any of the in-terrogators employed by the Gestapo in the nineteen forties extracted from their victims the names of those with whom their parents and grandparents had consorted in the eighteen nine-ties. This was common form with the Inquisition. When Hélis de Mazerolles, a Parfaite and a member of an important family in the Languedoc, was interrogated on August 5th, 1243, she

73

was obliged to reveal whom she had visited as a little girl between forty and fifty years previously. The penal code of the Inquisition was highly retrospective. This is not an isolated case. This pattern of interrogation reproduces itself regularly in the Inquisitorial records. The accused is taken back to childhood with Freudian regularity.

The Inquisitors relied largely on the work of informers. This showed itself in its simplest form in its attempts to extract information inculpating others from people already undergoing interrogation. But the majority of the people thus interrogated found themselves in this predicament as a result of the efforts of earlier informers. The victim was not allowed to know the names of the individuals who had denounced him. The Inquisition expressed concern lest informants be exposed to reprisals from the populace. This mechanism of secret denunciation was an ideal method of disposing of those against whom one had a personal grudge. It was also a convenient method of cancelling out debts one had incurred. The Inquisitors could liquidate the whole affair. Those accused by the Inquisition were not allowed a lawyer or to call witnesses in their defence.

Sometimes, like the Gestapo, the Inquisitors made mass arrests. In the early years of the fourteenth century the whole village of Montaillou was arrested but in this case, owing to the relative enlightenment of Jacques Fournier, the punishments inflicted were not great.

The prisons used by the Inquisition accommodated not only those sentenced to long term or to life imprisonment but also those awaiting further interrogation. It was sometimes the practice to commit the accused to prison, after an inconclusive session of interrogation, in order to see if a second session would have better results in a different atmosphere. One of these prisons was the celebrated Mur at Carcassonne. Here was practised what seems a most enlightened and modern procedure. The accused, if he were married, could be visited by his wife and relatives. This pleasing concern to maintain the sanctity of family life under unfortunate circumstances enabled the Inquisition to make further notes as to his family connections. Should he later be convicted he lived according to the regulations prescribed for the permanent residents. He lived alone in a cell chained to the wall until he died.

Though its exponents were sincere in their conviction that they were working for Christ and administering the law, the real success of the Inquisition was that it developed into a systematised instrument of terror unequalled in human history. Over a huge area those innocent of heresy were as liable to suffer as those addicted to it. What it aimed at doing was to create an atmosphere in which Catharism simply could not live. That the latter lasted even as long as it did is proof of the toughness of its adherents. It is undeniable that the havoc wrought by the Inquisition far exceeds that achieved by the Ogpu and the Gestapo. The Jews and Poles were not wholly exterminated either actually or politically. In just short of a century Catharism, which had threatened the very existence of Catholicism in the Midi, had been reduced to a handful of clandestine activists. When one considers that Hitler had at his command all the devices for the dissemination of information and defamatory propaganda, the achievements of the Inquisition are truly impressive. Every repressive system of secret police in the modern world should pay suitable acknowledgements to its great predecessor and prototype.

Catharism died, or went underground in other forms, early in the fourteenth century. The Inquisition continued for more than six hundred years. It must be admitted that, after the persecution of the Templars in the early fourteenth century, it lost some of the mole-like conscientiousness and ardent ferocity it had displayed in the first decades after its inception by Dominic.

The penal code of the Inquisition was also directed against the dead. Where the latter were proved to have been heretic their skeletons were tried and condemned. It is interesting that the technique of condemnation was the same as that employed for the living. No witnesses could be called in the defence of the deceased. The Inquisitors were well drilled in their logic though a little inelastic. The bones of heretics were disinterred and publicly burned. The vision of the Inquisition was also revealed in the scope of its retrospective legislation.

The possessions of the accused, as inherited by his living descendants, were also confiscated. One begins to see more clearly why the Inquisitors were concerned to obtain the names of those with whom the living accused had consorted half a century previously.

There is nothing conjectural in what I have said. The Inquisitorial records are accessible. A number of folios were studied and documented in the past by Limborch, Guiraud and others. A great deal of work has been done in the last few years. Perhaps the most magisterial work of this nature is that achieved by Duvernoy in his editing of the Inquisitorial records of Jacques Fournier. What is undoubted is that these records were voluminous and that in spite of the destruction of archives at the Revolution and at other periods of upheaval in French history they can still provide us with a vast source of information. It is remarkable that the full investigation of the whole matter has been left to the present day, but then the extermination of the Cathars was accompanied not only by forgetfulness of them but by the vilification of what little memory remained to us.

The Inquisition was spinsterish about the actual liquidation of the culpable. They were concerned only with the examination of his case. When he had been found guilty he was handed over to the secular arm. He was burnt by the secular authorities. Where torture was necessary to extract confessions, this was also left to the secular arm but the Inquisitors could be, and were, present. It should be emphasised that the accused was to some extent protected by the laws of the Inquisition. It was laid down that he should not be subjected to torture more than once. This was a handicapping clause, the effects of which were intelligently minimised by the Inquisitors. Where it was beneficial to the soul of the accused, they advised repetition of the torture, on the grounds that the further applications of persuasion were separate acts but performed in the same session.

However much the matter has been forgotten, both purposefully and involuntarily, there can be no doubt that the Inquisition was established to combat Catharism, and that it was at its most efficient in dealing with what to it was the great heresy. Certainly the Vaudois, to be regarded from some points of view

76

as precursors of Protestantism, were also persecuted by it but they were never, by the nature and degree of dissemination of their doctrines, such a menace to Rome as the Cathars.

It is a sad irony that near Fanjeaux, one of the strongest centres of Catharism, a notice board bears the inscription 'To the Dominican Holy Sites.' Certainly St. Dominic lived in this town but he was a late arrival compared with the Cathars. It is a strange commentary on human nature that the contemporary world prefers to celebrate the grand Inquisitor rather than the exponents of one of the world's oldest and most refined philosophies.

The principal house in Fanjeaux, once the residence of Guillaume de Durfort, the Cathar troubadour, is now a Catholic home for maladjusted girls. Other times, other customs.

CHAPTER TEN

Anyone with a smattering of knowledge of Catharism has heard of Montségur. It is popularly thought that the surrender of the fortress was the virtual end of Catharism. This is erroneous. Duvernoy has demonstrated clearly that the faith had a positive and vigorous recrudescence at the end of the thirteenth and the beginning of the fourteenth centuries. At the time of Montségur it had at least another sixty years to go. Nevertheless the fall of Montségur had two crucial results. It removed the heart and soul of Catharism. By the late 1230s Montségur had become not only a refuge but the main administrative centre. It was the place to which the Parfaits and others gravitated from the areas where persecution was most intense. It was the sole remaining refuge of those requiring instruction in the higher flights of Catharism. This was necessarily so because in the last few years of its existence its senior bishops and deacons were centred on it. In addition the fall of Montségur destroyed for ever the hope of an independent civilisation for the Languedoc. It was not that the capitulation was an important event in the military history of the Albigensian wars. To all intents and purposes the fate of the Languedoc had been decided already at the Treaty of Meaux. The siege of Montségur was only important in the secular history of the Languedoc because it, and the events leading to it, provided Raymond VII with his last opportunity to resist the extortions of destiny.

Montségur has become such a site of legend that before describing the siege and the events which led up to it, it is necessary to say something of the place itself.

It is almost certain that from time immemorial the pog, or summit, of the mountain was a religious site. The area around it is rich in relics of earlier religions. Near Morency, a few miles from Montségur, there is a druidical altar and a cross with an extraordinary amalgamation of Christian and pre-Christian motives including a figure 8 and the face of a pagan god. This cross stands close to the celebrated stone of Morency. Both are sited on a hill in such a way as to look directly across to the summit of Montségur.

In the caves of the Ariège, in the neighbourhood of Montségur, there is evidence of the practice of the cult of Mithras. These caves were used later for meditation by the Cathars. It is possible that Montségur was associated with another cult preoccupied with the rising and setting of the sun. It is held with great confidence to have been a Manichean holy place. It was characteristic of this religion that prayers should be said at the rising and going down of the sun, and particularly at the times of the equinox. There was a château on the summit here long before the twelfth century. The building we see now is the ruin of that reconstructed by Raymond de Perella in the early years of the thirteenth century.

Experts such as Fernand Niel assert positively that Montségur, and another Cathar citadel called Queribus were, or had been, centres of sun worship. Both châteaux have an arrangement of archeres, slits in the masonry through which arrows could be fired, and interior structures so ordered that the sun alighted on them at the religiously significant hours of the day or season.

When Guilhabert de Castres approached Raymond de Perella in the early years of the thirteenth century, did he foresee that the remote site of Montségur could serve as a last and secure rallying place for Cathars if things went adversely for them? If he did he was considering Montségur as a centre and a refuge rather than a fortress. Certainly when one looks at the pog from the road below one wonders how it came to fall and how the Navarrese who climbed its eastern face managed to penetrate into its interior. But to arrive at the summit is to doubt if it was ever intended for military use. Its seeming impregnability is more a question of site than structure. The living space within its walls is limited. There is really no room for a sizeable garrison and for the number of Cathar Parfaits and croyants who lived there at different times. What fortress was handicapped by having what, for military purposes, was a quite unnecessary second port of entry? This can still be seen in the wall opposite that which frames the main entrance. Though the word Montségur was to become immortal because of its association with the siege it is more likely that it was conceived of as a rallying point and a resting place for Cathar adepts and their acolytes in an inaccessible area away from the main roads and the marching armies.

Certainly it was a busy centre of pilgrimage. These constant comings and goings were intensified in the years before the siege. The depositions made before the Inquisition record the names of those who visited and stayed in the château. It was constantly visited by members of the noble families of the modern departments of Aude and Ariège. These people were not pilgrims in the Catholic sense of the word. There were no relics to venerate and those who went there did so to receive instruction from, and to live in the atmosphere radiated by, the Parfaits.

There is no doubt that with the passage of time the military significance of Montségur increased. It acquired a garrison commanded in its last years by Pierre-Roger de Mirepoix. The latter was a *faidit*, a landless knight outlawed for heresy. He lived at Montségur in the company of other nobles in a similar predicament. What touched off the siege was the affair at Avignonet, which took place in May 1242. It was then that two Inquisitors, Guillaume Arnaud and Pierre Seila, were due to open a session of the Holy Office at Avignonet. The region was still saturated in heresy. The practice of anonymous denunciation was so well established that any sitting of the Inquisitors was regarded with terror by the whole population. No one could be certain that, no matter how undeviating his orthodoxy, his name might not appear in the Inquisitorial records. The Inquisitors stayed in the house of Raymond d'Alfaro. This man, who was an official of the Count of Toulouse, informed Pierre-Roger de Mirepoix of the arrival of the Inquisitors. Pierre-Roger set off from Montségur with a troop of knights and sergeants-at-arms. They were met at Gaja-la-Selve by another detachment led by Pierre de Mazerolles. A number of men chosen from both parties set off for Avignonet. On arrival they were met at the outskirts of the town by a servant of d'Alfaro. They were conducted by him to the latter's house where the Inquisitors were duly despatched.

Catholic histories have had no hesitation in describing this as an odious murder, as indeed it was in the sense that all violence is deplorable. But it is easy across the gulf of seven centuries to look back on an isolated crime in a sea of bloodshed and to strike pious attitudes about it. Indeed it is unnecessary to look back more than thirty years to find its exact equivalent. The Inquisitors were liquidated on the eve of one of their murderous sessions. It was as if two members of the Gestapo had been bumped off because their continued existence threatened the lives of many innocent people in the area to which they had been posted. The knights responsible for this deed were no doubt, with their families and dependants, on the list of suspects which meant, according to Inquisitorial law, that they were due for condemnation. Had they operated under exactly similar circumstances in the France, Holland or Poland of thirty years ago they would still be described as heroes of the Resistance. Looking back, self-consciously and a little hypocritically from times of somewhat greater security, we can at least say this was an act of self-protection, perhaps of social justice, conducted as part of an underground war with the aim of protecting the oppressed from greater horrors. In any case the Inquisitors concerned have since been canonised. A resurrected Nazism could still do the same for Himmler and Goering.

There can be no doubt that Raymond VII connived at the murder of the Inquisitors. It occurred after all at the house of one of his agents. He was informed of it the morning after by the commander of the Montségur garrison through the intermediary of Isarn de Fanjeaux. Avignonet did not help him at all. His affairs went from bad to worse. His few lukewarm allies divested themselves of his embarrassing company. He submitted again to Blanche of Castille in October 1242. When he renewed his homage to her the following Spring he undertook to extirpate heresy from his territories. Blanche was desperately determined to reduce Montségur, 'the dragon's head of heresy.'

81

The recruitment of the army was entrusted to Hugues de Arcis and Pierre-Amiel, the Archbishop of Narbonne. It is interesting how, throughout the Albigensian campaigns, the Church was identified so closely with the armed forces in the actual pursuit of war.

There are certain curious features of the siege. At one stage in the proceedings the assailants were causing considerable damage to the defenders by the installation of an engine of war on one of the slopes near the fortress. This stone-throwing monster was the favourite brain child of a bishop supervising the besiegers' artillery. After this engine had caused considerable damage the situation was equalised by the appearance among the defenders of a noted engineer, Bertrand de la Baccaralia. There is little doubt that he was sent at the instigation of the Count of Toulouse. It is also clear that people were able to enter the beleaguered fortress without too much difficulty. This could be attributable simply to the efforts of skilled scouts and sympathetic peasants who knew the paths through the dense shrubs which on certain aspects still invest the summit. At the same time it is clear that there were Cathar sympathisers in the investing army.

The siege lasted ten months. In the early Spring of 1244 the Crusaders effected an entry to the fortress. Anyone visiting it today and standing at the point where the entry was effected will wonder how a force climbing such precipitous and dangerous slopes could have approached the castle walls unobserved. Perhaps the sentinels were asleep. Perhaps the defenders simply assumed that no one would risk such an operation. Perhaps there was a traitor in the château. In any case it became clear to the commander of the garrison that all further resistance was useless. A surrender was negotiated to take place after a truce of a fortnight.

This is where the mystery intensifies. Why a gap of a fortnight? This was quite unprecedented in the Middle Ages. After a negotiated surrender, even when the latter was honoured by the investing army, the best the besieged could hope for was a day's respite. The terms were also surprisingly generous. The garrison were free to depart, retaining their arms. This was not unknown in the Middle Ages but that it should have been accorded and honoured in a war which was a long atrocity is surprising in the extreme. The Parfaits and the obstinate cro-yants were of course to be surrendered. It may seem singularly unheroic and cold-hearted that the garrison commander, Pierre-Roger de Mirepoix, was prepared to march out with his soldiers and leave the Cathars to their fate. The issue is not as simple as that. Raymond de Perella, the owner of the castle, Pierre-Roger de Mirepoix, and the Parfaits, of whom Bertrand Marty was at this stage the most influential, had undergone the rigours of the siege together. There is no evidence of any differ-ence of policy between them. Also the relationship between the Cathars and the soldiers who defended them remained cordial to the end. Before the garrison marched out they were given presents of spices, money and food by the Parfaits. Certainly the latter submitted without protest to their own fate and it is clear that they agreed with the surrender.

There is a further and most striking fact which illuminates for us the attitude of Pierre-Roger de Mirepoix. After the truce he arranged for four Parfaits to be lowered by ropes from the walls of the castle. These men were destined for the caves of the Upper Ariège and were carrying with them the so-called treas-ure of the Cathars. (During the siege there had been two earlier expeditions connected with the disposal of the treasure.) It was arranged that the fugitives should light a fire on the Bidorte, the mountain across the valley from the pog of Montségur, to an-nounce that they had passed safely through the enemy lines. The signal was duly received.

Historians have given different dates for the escape of the Parfaits with the treasure. It probably took place the night after their confrères were burnt at the stake. The garrison, without the Cathars, marched out on the fourteenth of March. Pierre-Roger stayed on with a handful of supporters, ostensibly to see that the conditions of the capitulation were observed. He was probably concerned with the security of those civilians who denied they were Cathars. The latter were burnt on the six-teenth.

In lowering the four Parfaits down the sides of the château,

which must have remained under surveillance from the besiegers, Pierre-Roger was taking an appalling risk. He was deceiv-
ing the Crusaders and in so doing jeopardising the conditions of
the truce and his own personal safety and that of his family and
followers. Two relatives had been handed over as hostages to
the enemy.

The whole flavour of the fortnight's truce suggests that it
gave the Cathars time to make certain preparations vital to
them. The disposal of the treasure is what most excites the imagination but there is another factor of equal importance. It is
reasonable that during this time the Parfaits and croyants, by
prayer and meditation, prepared themselves for death. Certainly at this time many, and not only the severely wounded,
received the Consolamentum. It has been argued that the
period of the truce coincided with the Spring feast of Manes, the
founder of the Manichean faith, but the evidence is presumptive. Catharism harked back far more directly to primitive
Christianity than many have imagined. One cannot escape the
conclusion that the fortnight's respite before the implementa-
tion of the surrender was something which suited the interests
of both the Cathars and the garrison, as well as their assailants.
Among the latter there may still have been quite influential
sympathisers with the Cathar cause.

The Parfaits were dragged down and burnt, it is said on the
lower slopes of the mountain. A small monument indicates the
area where it is supposed that they suffered. It is possible that
this is wrongly sited and that the place of martyrdom was a level
space lower and to the right as one descends the hill. Among
those who perished were the wife, daughter and mother-in-law
of Raymond de Perella, the owner of the Château. He himself
had not received the Consolamentum but his Cathar sympa-
thies were evident and he appeared later before the Inquisition.
Two hundred Parfaits were burnt at Montségur.

What was the Montségur treasure? Catharism and the cult
of the Graal have this in common, that for both deliverance is
not by sacraments but by the development of a higher consciousness and a new vision, but there is concrete evidence that
the Graal legend had roots in the Cathar country. None of this

justifies for a moment the speculation that the treasure of Montségur was a sacred chalice. Such preoccupations are for the hectically romantic and do not merit discussion. It is surely inconceivable that the chalice still existed in the thirteenth century. Even had it done so it is difficult to believe it would have been excessively valued. A faith which did not build churches, rejected sacraments, and was uninterested in holy relics was not likely to have concerned itself unduly with an object of this nature. To believe that the treasure was the Graal is to subscribe to a romantic view of Catharism which obscures its interpretation. That the Graal, that is to say a chalice, should appear on the wall of a cave in the Ariège is easily explicable. The chalice, with the dove and the rose, is one of the visionary patterns which have appeared regularly to Cathars and other Dualists before and since.

Among the more instructed it is assumed that the treasure consisted of sacred writings. Here again the question should be approached with caution. One is always a little suspicious of the usefulness and existence of so-called sacred books of limited circulation among the initiates. It has always been characteristic of esoteric cults throughout the ages that essential wisdom has been transmitted by word of mouth. The oral method is preferred where its exponents are sufficiently wise to know that prayers, meditations and rites should be prescribed to fit the different temperaments of different aspirants. The Parfaits were too skilled in the management of their flock, and too many were doctors, to over emphasise the importance of sacred writings. Nevertheless two or three of the Parfaits who had delved deep into philosophy by means of what I suppose would now be called transcendental meditation, committed to parchment what they had seen and experienced and knew to be true. Guilhabert de Castres certainly wrote a record of the basic and undeviating truths which he had experienced.

As well as frankly esoteric communications the treasure consisted of rare manuscripts. These included some of the lost gospels. It is commonly believed hat the Cathars possessed a special version of the gospel according to St. John. There is no real evidence for this. Had they possessed it they would certainly have used it. Perhaps those who hold this view are confusing this hypothetical amended gospel with La Cene Secrète a fascinating document which is, however, no more than an imaginary conversation in which Christ enlightens John as to the real nature of His mission. Certainly the ordinary Gospel according to St. John was of major importance to the Cathars. Each Parfait carried a copy constantly with him. The first chapter, and in particular the first seventeen verses, were regarded as of especial importance. Included in the Cathar treasure was also a collection of rare but not necessarily unique books. These included the works of Greek philosophers from Pythagoras to Plato. Democritus and Epicurus were among their number. The neo-Platonists and, in particular, Plotinus and Porphyry, were well represented. So were the Alexandrine School. The works of Valentinus and Basilides were included in the Cathar library. It is commonly held that there was no great outflow of classical literature from Byzantium until the fall of Constantinople in 1453. This is quite erroneous because Averrhoës, born at Cordoba, was making his commentaries on Aristotle in the twelfth century. There was a considerable dispersal of scholars and literature from Byzantium after the fourth crusade in 1204, another horrifying episode instigated by Innocent III. Actual manuscripts of classical and neo-classical writers cannot have been common in the thirteenth century. There was no place, outside their country of origin, where they were more likely to accumulate than the Languedoc. The latter provided the most literate and tolerant civilisation extant. It was also on the great trade routes from the Levant. The Cathars were aware of their indebtedness to their classical and neo-classical roots. One can indeed say that Catharism leaned steeply towards the Greek and away from the Jewish origins of Christianity.

The treasure of the Cathars must, in part, have included money. Like any other organisation they could not have functioned without it. Though they built no churches there were Cathar houses where the constantly travelling Parfaits could sometimes find repose. Payment for horses is mentioned in the records and must have been a considerable expense in view of the distances covered by the Parfaits, some of whom travelled on horseback. There was also the upkeep of the convents for women. What was probably the biggest expense was the maintenance of the workshops where young artisans were instructed in weaving, leather-making, and in other trades. Unlike the Church, the Cathar faith did not rely for its existence on extortions from the people of tithes and other obligatory offerings. Legacies to the Cathars were the rule among the faithful. The Cathars do not appear to have been short of funds. There were volunteers who served them as carriers and receivers of money. For centuries people have searched around Montségur, along the slopes of Saint Barthelemy and in the valley of the Ariège for the Cathar treasure. It is not likely that future investigators will come up with a big haul.

The last instalment of the Cathar treasure, evacuated from Montségur at the end of the siege, found refuge at Château d'Usson. It consisted of precious manuscripts including one devoted to the art of healing. These simply disappeared in the course of centuries.

CHAPTER ELEVEN

The fall of Montségur makes a sad, dramatic and fitting moment to let fall the curtain on the Albigensian tragedy. In actual fact there were several further acts in the drama which was still being actively played as late as the first years of the fourteenth century. Quéribus, in the southern extremity of the Corbières, was still a nest of heretics as late as 1255. In that year an expedition was mounted against it at the instigation of Blanche of Castille. As in the case of Montségur, there is a mystery attached to the fall of Quéribus. We do not know whether it was acquired by treachery or as a result of a parley.

This was by no means the end of Catharism. It has often been said that, from that time onwards, all that existed of the faith was a hunted peasantry in the caves and mountains of the Upper Ariège, and a devoted and secret minority in such places as Albi, Carcassonne and Toulouse. Certainly there were outbreaks directed against the Inquisition in the two latter cities. The works of Duvernoy and Nelli have dispelled the illusion that Catharism died in the mid-thirteenth century. It enjoyed a St. Martin's Summer in the Upper Ariège in the latter half of that century. At this time the constitution of its priesthood was changed. It no longer attracted such a large proportion of the nobility. Many had been killed in the wars and many were in exile as proscribed outlaws. It may well have been that current events did not incline such men to a lifetime of non-resistance. The number of aristocratic entrants was also reduced by the fact that in this time of war and massacre less women became Parfaites. The daughters of the minor nobility had previously provided many entrants to the priesthood. At the end of the century only one Parfaite is recorded as still at work.

It cannot be said that the last Parfaits were recruited from

uncultured backgrounds. A number were lawyers and cultivated merchants. Pierre Autier, who achieved miracles of devotion and heroism throughout the Languedoc till his death at the
stake in 1310, was a lawyer from Ax-les-Thermes. Loyalty to
the faith was still to be found in all classes of society.

Though I have emphasised the social background of the
priesthood it should be clearly understood that social position
played no part in the selection of Parfaits. Purity of life and
capability of development were the main requirements. At all
times the Parfaits were recruited from all classes. Bertrand
Marty, who at the time of the siege of Montségur was incomparably the most influential of the Parfaits, was almost certainly of humble origin.

If one wishes to do the impossible and estimate when Catharism died as an open and living force, the date of Autier's martyrdom is as good as any. Other Parfaits continued to exist and
preach after his day. Guillaume Belibaste survived till 1321,
when he was given away by an informer. He was burnt at the
charming village of Villerouge-Termènes.

What happened to Catharism after 1320 or thereabouts? Did
it die out utterly or did it persist in an underground form? The
question is best posed otherwise. What happened to the eternal
current of Dualism, to the Gnose which insists that the
psyche enters the soul at conception with its memory of past
lives, that it is purified in a series of incarnations, and that in
the universe there are two eternal principles of good and evil.

At the time when Catharism was on its deathbed another
organisation was suddenly and catastrophically persecuted
by the King of France and the Inquisition. We know little of
the exact beliefs of the Templars, though in France there is a
surprisingly copious literature on the subject. There are indi-
cations of some connection between the Cathars and the
Templars. A large number of Templar Knights were
recruited from the Languedoc. There was an influx of recruits
in the mid-thirteenth century when the Albigensian wars
were to all intents and purposes over. It is significant that the
immensely powerful and ubiquitous order of the Temple took
no part in the Crusade against the Albigensians. This is all

the more significant because the Templars were not under the jurisdiction of the local bishops and archbishops but directly responsible to the Pope. As we have seen Innocent III was the main instigator of the Crusade. It is strange that more effort was not asked or offered by them. For a long time it has been suggested that, after Montségur, there was an infiltration of avowed Cathars into the Order of the Temple. I personally regarded the historical evidence as interesting, presumptive but not conclusive. Evidence from discarnate sources leaves no doubt that it is true.

The Temple died a more sudden death than Catharism. The mass arrests ordered by Philippe le Bel for the same day in different parts of France took place in 1307. Jacques de Molay, the grandmaster of the Temple, died at the stake in 1314, the year before Pierre Autier's martyrdom. The violent liquidation of the Templars and the final cleaning up of the Cathars occurred at the same period of history. Their dates of birth were also similar. The Order of the Temple was instituted at the beginning of the heretical twelfth century.

The directly historical evidence is inadequate to enable us to speak with accuracy of the beliefs of the Templars. In the case of the Cathars we can read between the innumerable lines of the Inquisitorial records. With the Templars we have no detailed report of what they said under interrogation by the Inquisitors. The procés verbal reports only the proceedings of the secular court after the accused had been softened up by the Holy Office. The Templars were beyond doubt Dualists. Their Dualism had possibly a strong Gnostic derivation.

Just as the wars against the Albigeois deteriorated into a scramble for territory and riches, the campaign against the Templars can be comprehensively explained by Phillipe le Bel's desire for money. His exchequer was embarassed at the time and the richness of the Order of the Temple was proverbial. Nevertheless it is undeniable that the Templars were contaminated by heresy and as such a target for the secular and clerical authorities. At their trials the most dramatic indictment was that the initiates were required to spit on the Cross. Learned authorities on the subject have suggested that this was a stylised re-echo of Peter denying Christ three times and, as such, an act of devotion. Others have regarded it as a crude initiation ceremony of a military order. By far the most likely explanation is that the Templars had similar ideas on the Incarnation to those of the Cathars. The latter could not accept the orthodox Christian interpretation. To them the Son of God could not be imprisoned, and could not die, in matter. The Cathar destestation of the crucifixion was notorious. The Templars' contempt for the Cross was merely another version of it.

There are many sympathetic references to heresy in the works of Dante. The Catholic writer Aroux has elucidated this better than anybody. It has been suggested that Dante's lost Beatrice referred to the Cathar Church which had perished. Why, after her death, should the poet have addressed himself to the head of the Holy Roman Empire? Why should the latter have been especially interested in the death in her teens of a Florentine bourgeoise? The Emperor's heretical leanings were well known and Dante was symbolising the loss of someone who perhaps never existed. To others the lost Beatrice represents the disappearance of the Gospels in the vernacular. Dante was strongly influenced by the Troubadour poetry which was contemporaneous with Catharism in the Languedoc and which often expressed in a veiled way the truths of the latter religion. Certainly, on his own admission, he hesitated before writing in what he described as the languages of the *si* or the *oc*, that is to say Tuscan or Languedoc. It is possible that Dante's use of the latter term to describe the tongue of the Troubadours is the first reference to the langue d'oc as a language as distinct from a region. We have no candid statement of the poet's beliefs which would enable us to say positively that he was a Cathar. In his day the reaction to the persecution of the Templars must have been more acute and it is more probable that his heretical leanings were tilted in the direction of their Order.

After the disappearance of Catharism and the Temple at the beginning of the fourteenth century what outlet was there for those of Dualist tendency? One thing we can say with certainty. By this time the Dualists of Europe had learnt that the open profession of their opinions was so hazardous as to be impracticable. What characterises these persecutions of Dualism is the thoroughness with which they were conducted and the skill with which the persecutors managed for centuries to convey that there was something sinister about the faiths for which the martyrs died. The cult of Mithras, of Manes, and the Cathars were each in turn exterminated and vilified to a degree far exceeding what the Huguenots were later to suffer from the Catholics, and the Jews from the Nazis. The Templars did not fare too badly in Aragon and Castille and escaped unscathed but under a different name in Portugal. Certainly in the succeeding centuries Dualism went underground. Some of its principles were practised by the Rosicrucians but under conditions of such secrecy as may seem ludicrous to the uniformed sceptic. As in resistance movements in the last war, the Rosicrucians were unfamiliar with the majority of those who belonged to their order and were only known to their immediate associates. In view of the previous persecutions to which Dualism had been subjected, these precautions cannot be described as superfluous. It is traditional that the Rosicrucian movement arose in Germany in a family where a monk from Narbonne had been appointed as tutor. Nobody can prove that this is so but the way so many heresies are accredited with origins in the Languedoc or Pyrenees is in itself of some significance. Even Michelet quotes the story of the Templar knights who rose from their graves on the anniversary of the martyrdom of Jacques Mornay. He sites this legend at Gavarnie in the Pyrenees. It is reasonable to consider that some legends persist because they contain within them a particle of truth. Perhaps it is best to regard Dualism as analogous to a repressed impulse. It passes from memory but continues to exert its influence in different directions below the conscious level.

The Alchemists come next in the secret line of succession. The claim that they were concerned with the transmutation of base metals to gold was the window dressing for an esoteric meaning. The latter implied the self-purification without benefit of masses and sacraments which characterised Dualism throughout the centuries. The alchemists took the precaution of writing much of their literature in cipher. There is no reason to assume that this was in order to provide the faithful with an educative esoteric exercise. It was more likely designed to hide from the world that they were indulging in unorthodox beliefs which might well expose them to the charge of heresy. Not all the alchemists' beliefs and practices were Dualist but the influence of the latter was obviously strong.

It has been suggested that modern Freemasonry follows in the same Dualist tradition. Generally speaking this claim has been grossly exaggerated. It is difficult to imagine mediaeval Dualists having anything in common with either British bourgeois conservative masonry or with the so-called Leftish Grand Orient Lodge in France. There are modern forms of Masonry which, in their concern for the material, are the complete negation of Catharism. Nevertheless the derivation of certain varieties of modern, though not contemporary, masonry, in the mediaeval freemasons and the Temple cannot be dismissed out of hand. Certainly a non-ritualistic, Dualist variety of freemasonry was being practised in France as late as 1850.

With the enormous resurgence of interest in Catharism can one say that there are consciously practising Cathars in our time? One can answer this, in a limited sense, in the affirmative. Déodat Roché and his school, in their interpretation of the transcendental motives of Catharism, are surely doing more than raking the embers. In explaining its significance to modern audiences they are performing to a limited degree what the Parfaits did in the thirteenth century. Their mouthpiece is the *Cahiers d'Etudes Cathares*, a journal which can be regarded as a twentieth century statement of Dualism. This circle is also very interested in anthroposophy. Much of Steiner's teaching resembles Catharism and is also in accordance with Gnostic doctrine.

Catharism persists in the folklore of the regions where it was once rampant. Professor Nelli deals with this in his book *La Vie Quotidienne des Cathares*. He gave me a recent example. Two farmers were out shooting in the Corbières and flushed a partridge. One raised his gun and the other immediately begged him to desist because he felt sure that the bird was his uncle.

This, of course, is an example of a debased form of Catharism. There is no evidence that the Cathars believed in the transmigration of souls from men to animals, and vice versa. There is the celebrated story of the Parfait who recognised his pre-existence as a horse, but this is not to be taken as typical. The beliefs of Catharism varied somewhat according to the regions in which it was practised. I understand from Lawrence Durrell that fragments of Catharism are to be found in the folklore of the Cevennes. The latter is known to us mostly as a hotbed of Protestantism but the items of folklore predate the existence of the Huguenots.

CHAPTER TWELVE

The culture, as well as the civilisation, of the twelfth and thirteenth century Languedoc, was indisputably ahead of any-
where else in Europe. The reputation of the former rests chiefly
on the contribution of the troubadour poets. Elsewhere there
were significant contemporary poets like Chrétien de Troyes
but where could one discover such a nest of singing birds as that
represented by the Languedoc of the period under discussion?
Even seen across the veil of translation the troubadour achievement is magnificent in the elegance, significance and meaning
of its poetry and in the number of poets engaged in its production. Raymond de Miraval, Pierre Cardenal, Bernard de
Ventadour, Pierre Vidal, Rambaut de Vacqueiras, Marcabrun
– all these are names to conjure with.

When one considers also that the poets limited themselves to
set forms one is all the more amazed at their achievement. They
restricted themselves to such forms because to some extent a
proportion of these poems are of the nature of conundrums. A
secret of esoteric significance is hidden in them. The poems run
a set coursé. Then there is a twist in its tail and we are carried to
another plane of meaning. C.S. Lewis wrote of the immense significance of the troubadour contribution and discussed its relation with the Renaissance. Had it not been for the Crusade
and the subsequent wars and persecutions, the culture of the
Languedoc could have anticipated the Renaissance in Italy by
more than two centuries. The background was there and the
raw material was rich. The influence of the troubadours was
immense, not only on Dante but on his contemporaries and
successors. Cavalcanti and others have affinities with their
models in the Languedoc and Provence. Nita de Pierrefeu has
demonstrated the likenesses between the Italian *fideli d'amori*
and troubadour poetry.

It is of cardinal importance to study what affinities existed between the Cathars and the troubadours. Catholic writers tend to underestimate the contribution of what were surely the fathers of European poetry. What is more important is that apologists for the Church, and others, have refused to accept that the troubadour poetry and Catharism are related to each other. This is quite untenable. How could two such startling manifestations of culture occur at the same time and in a limited area without their being related to each other? To hold such an opinion is equivalent to saying that the teachings of Freud swept London in the nineteen twenties but had no influence on medicine or literature. There can be no doubt whatever that the two aspects of the same civilisation were linked with each other. The question is how much?

In many cases the noble houses which gave refuge to the Cathars also acted as hosts to the troubadours. The family which entertained the celebrated Pierre Vidal was also active in the Cathar cause. It cannot be said that Catharism obtrudes everywhere in troubadour poetry. Certainly there are five or six troubadour poets with distinct Cathar leanings which are clearly discernible in their writings. One practising and devoted Cathar is known to have been a troubadour. This was Guillaume de Durfort whose fidelity to Catharism led to his being dispossessed of his lands and who took refuge in Aragon.

What is transparently obvious in troubadour poetry is that much of it was anti-clerical. Some of the special category of abusive poems called Sirventes were more vituperative than the anti-clerical propaganda we have known in this century. But because so much troubadour poetry criticised and ridiculed the Catholic priesthood in general, and the hierarchy in particular, we cannot necessarily assume that its writers were Cathars. Such material is evidence only of the anti-Romanism of the Languedoc and of the freedom which existed, before the Crusades, to vilify the established religion.

Much of the verse of the troubadours is what at first sight we can call love poetry. Some of it may have been no more than that, but to dismiss it all as of this nature is fatuous in the extreme. The picture of the troubadour playing his guitar out-side a lady's window and supplicating her favours is a music hall myth. Troubadours of a lower quality, at a later date and in other countries, may have limited themselves in this way but those of the twelfth and thirteenth century Languedoc had a special function to perform. There were certain features of this poetry which make it inadmissible to infer that it was merely concerned with the human love of man for woman. Firstly the love celebrated was to an overwhelming degree either unre-quited or unattainable. The lady invoked was often of vastly superior social position to the poet. This was often so in fact. Bernard Ventadorn was the son of a baker. The famous Pierre Vidal was of humble origin. This neither prevented them ad-dressing their poetry to ladies of noble birth or being welcome in their houses. Secondly, the lady was almost always married. The suggestion that the troubadours devoted a whole intricate and esoteric system of poetry to the celebration of adultery *per se* does not make sense. It is completely unlikely that in the Middle Ages men of humble origin should consistently risk their position, prestige and perhaps their lives, in celebrating the theme of illicit relations with women of noble birth. It is inconceivable that men of different gifts and temperaments and living in different decades, should devote themselves so con-stantly to the poetic and spiritual celebration of adultery. This idea is all the more untenable in that the lady was so con-stantly remote and unattainable. It was indeed permissible to fall in love with someone the poet had not seen. In the light of what we shall see later this was not only allowable but logical. It is what, by tradition, happened to Geffroi Rudel. He fell in love with the Princess of Tripoli on the basis of a description he had heard of her. He met her only to die in her arms. This is a little too good to be true but it serves to give us an insight into the love for the distant and inaccessible princess.

What was behind the philosophy of the troubadours was not merely that love and marriage are two separate conditions but that bodily possession is also the death of love. The admired lady was not expected to surrender to the suppliant. The usual intention was that she should, if she intended to do so at all, bestow her favours slowly and piecemeal and that fulfilment should be long deferred and preferably without orgasm. There is evidence that the troubadours practised the form of passive sexuality known to Tantric Buddhism. What was implied was that love must live on its own tension. This was emphatically not the Freudian view of sublimation, that the sexual aspect of love is expressed and dissipated in poetry. What was implied was that by love the poet and, if possible, the object of his love, were lifted to a higher state of awareness. It suggested indeed that the love of woman was another aspect of the love of God. This was proved by the expectation that the poet should be spiritually elevated by his love and that he should show this in greater gentleness to his fellows, and, above all, in consideration for his inferiors.

The motive behind troubadour poetry was a plea for the higher evaluation of women. This expressed itself in what seemed a contempt for marriage, in that the poet addressed himself so exclusively to married women. But such aims were important in an age when, in spite of the enlightenment in the Languedoc, the marriages of the nobility were still to a great degree dynastic in intention. Nevertheless marriages and liasons between people of different class were more common in the Languedoc than elsewhere. The treatment of women is a good yardstick to measure any civilisation. The troubadours were driving the lesson home. They were saying in effect that so many marriages were loveless and involved, in their dynastic aims, the spiritual devaluation of women.

But what is of more significance is that the troubadour is invoking a female conception of the Holy Spirit. It is for this reason that in the majority of the love poems the woman is remote, inaccessible, difficult of access and to be approached with chastity. The troubadours were reaching back to the Mother Goddess of antiquity in her different forms.

It is too readily assumed that the Jewish conception of Monotheism, of the one God, was an enormous advance. Having reduced the number of deities to one it was inevitable, in a man-made world, that he should be thought of as masculine. God, the Jehovah of the Old Testament, was promptly endowed with all the masculine vices. He was ritualistic, aggressive and dominating. He exacted obedience and was merciless at its infraction. There is nothing fantastic about a female conception of the Holy Spirit. The woman principle expresses the virtues of compassion and love and a preference for the direct knowledge conferred by intuition over the disguised pugnacity of reasoning and logic. This idea of the long existing primordial feminine principle is a cardinal feature of the oldest and most durable Chinese philosophy, that of Lao Tse. It was resurrected long after the Middle Ages by Goethe with his conception of the Eternal Feminine. That this conception should have occurred in the Languedoc is not surprising. Catharism, with its inevitable blend of mysticism and logic, provided for modern Europe the unique spectacle of having, over a period of half a century, the same number of priestesses as priests.

This elevation of the woman principle to its rightful position not in, but above, the aspirations of this world, is revealed in those troubadour productions where the lady is referred to in the masculine gender.

Any attempt to explain these phenomena on Freudian lines can only be concerned with the thin epidermis of the problem presented, and can only reveal a complete misapprehension of the nature of the love extolled and practised by the troubadours.

In their poetry the troubadours were writing on both the exoteric and esoteric level. By the former one does not mean that one must accept the playing under the window and going into the bedroom concept. This is a fit basis for an Edwardian musical and for nothing else. The exoteric teaching is concerned with the status of women in this world and the degree to which the improvement in the social system depends on their emancipation. The esoteric interpretation is that which sees the recipient of the poet's favours as an allegory of the eternal and holy feminine principle. Is not something of the same interpretation to be read into the love of Dante for Beatrice? He only saw her rarely and he never spoke to her alone. He was separated from her by the gulf of decades. She died in her teens. Was not Dante living in his life and his poetry the possible fiction of Geoffroi

Rudel and his Princesse Lointaine? Some authorities on the troubadours, while accepting that they and the Cathars represent parallel strains in the same culture and civilisation, refuse to push the analogies too far. Nevertheless the link between them is closer than many admit. Much troubadour poetry is Catharism set to music. One should not expect too many concrete references. The form and constructions of the poems do not favour such techniques. It should also be remembered that, during and after the persecutions, the troubadours acted often as secret and sympathetic agents of Dualism. It was frequently their habit to carry a red rose when communicating something of esoteric and Dualistic significance and to refrain from doing so when they were singing a straight love song. Nor was it necessary, to sophisticated audiences, to drag in the beliefs and principles of Catharism in poems limited in size and form. A poet, transported by Keats' 'Beauty is truth, truth beauty' could write an ode to a primrose without dragging in the original quotation.

Though I do not regard Otto Rahn, author of *La Croisade contre le Graal*, as in any sense an authority, it is worth while mentioning one of his most stimulating conjectures. He suggested that the cultural structure of the mediaeval Languedoc resembled that of the Druids. The Druidic priests were analogous to the Parfaits and the bards to the troubadours. The Druids were forerunners of the Celtic Christian Church which in certain areas, as for example in the region corresponding to modern Cumberland, was strongly Dualist.

There are one or two obvious factors which reveal the link between the troubadours and Cathars. Surely the poet's devotion to a married woman re-echoes the Parfait's attitude to marriage, in that love, provided it has transcendental possibilities, is superior to what is based on the worldly contract of marriage, not recognised by the Cathars? And doesn't the troubadour's transmutation of sexuality reflect the Parfaits' exhortation to absolute chastity? These two likenesses simply cannot be coincidental.

In this country ignorance of the troubadours is, if anything, more complete than that of the Cathars. Certainly we have heard the name more often but we have debased its meaning more profoundly. In France itself, while interest in these poets is much greater, it cannot be said that the average Frenchman is bursting with knowledge of the subject. It is not only Catholic criticism which tends to see, in such forms as the Aubade, the young man celebrating his physical love for his mistress when he leaves her at dawn. Such criticism is less to be deplored than the ludicrous attempts made sometimes to play down the poetic achievements of the troubadours. Most Europeans with literary interests of any measureable depth would at the very least place them high among the founding fathers of European poetry.

CHAPTER THIRTEEN

Early Christianity was a markedly spiritist religion. Its adherents had great emanatory capacity displayed in healing and other psychic activities. By their nature they were distinguishable from the orthodox Catholic Christians and above all from the Catholic priesthood who were to succeed them. The Cathars were primitive Christians returned to a world where opinion had hardened against the spiritist phenomena manifested in the first three centuries after Christ. Because of their extra-sensory capacities the Cathars were regarded by the Inquisitors and the Roman priesthood as purveyors of magic. This was a crucial issue and a cardinal error. The Cathars and early Christians had no use for magic. They were spiritist without being in the least inclined to witchcraft, sorcery and magic. The Cathars for their part regarded the Catholic Church as saturated in magic. The Holy Sacrament, venerated by the faithful through the teaching of transubstantiation as an awesome and sacred bestowal of grace from on high was, to the Cathars, the continuance of a depraved expression of 'the king must be sacrificed' mythology. This question of magic is the ultimate watershed in the classification of religions. There are those, like Romans and Anglicans, who continue, and often with considerable benefit to their devotees, the primitive magic of earlier cults, and those, like Cathars, for whom what seems to be magical, like healing and prophecy, is merely a byproduct of the make-up of the individual.

Have we any other evidence separating off primitive Christianity from the Roman international theocracy which was to replace it? The Cathars held that this separation occurred at the crucifixion itself and argued that the devil exercised his influence on Christianity at this stage. The theory of a son of God incarnate in the flesh and dying on the cross was merely a refinement of a mythological concept. To the Cathars the primitive Christians of the first two centuries after Christ were a different kind of being from those who later constituted the Church rendered legal by Constantine. The Cathars claimed to be a resurgence of primitive Christianity. They continued the laying on of hands and the kiss of peace which had been practised by their fore-runners. They continued also the simple commemoration of Christ in the breaking of bread and the drinking of wine which was celebrated round a table as at the last supper, and in the course of which they met as brethren and expressed without set prayers their thankfulness for what had been revealed to them through Christ. This simple act of commemoration was also a continuance of a similar rite practised by the followers of Mithras. During the brutal persecution of the latter by the Christians, now emancipated by the edict of Constantine, it was alleged that the followers of Mithras had stolen the Christian sacrament. That the simple Mithraic ceremony had preceded the birth of Christ by centuries appears to have been regarded as irrelevant.

The question poses itself sharply; if Catharism was the resurgence of primitive Christianity, and if at the same time it was Dualist, can we therefore regard primitive Christianity as an episode in the history of Dualism? This conception fits in well enough with the view of those scholars for whom the Hellenic roots of Christianity are more important than the Judaic. There is plenty of evidence of Dualist tendencies in Greek philosophy from Pythogoras onwards. This is revealed chiefly in the belief in a reincarnating soul and in the calamity of being imprisoned in matter. So far as I know there is no complete triple-based statement of Dualism in pre-Christian Hellenic sources. There are those who point with confidence to references to reincarnation in the New Testament. It never seems to me that they are particularly convincing, but then the basic sacred writings of Christianity are remarkably sparse unless one still subscribes to the untenable view that the Old Testament as a whole is related to the teachings of Christ.

Compared with Buddhism the Gospels are very unclear as to the basic articles of Christian belief. There is nowhere any equivalent to Buddha's statement that life is suffering, that suffering is due to attachment and the latter to desire. Because of the poetic vision of Christ we are left to assemble the pieces together from a collection of parables and sayings requiring translation at the esoteric level. The sources of official Christianity and Dualism are the same. It is up to us to decide how we translate them. I myself am not satisfied that there is a plethora of Dualist references in the Gospels. With the Pauline writings we are on firmer ground. Paul has a clear conception of evil as a positive force and indicates that we are fighting not against men but against principalities and powers of darkness. There is no doubt whatever that he saw Christianity in its spiritist aspect. His conception of bodies corruptible and incorruptible ties up with the Cathar idea that the good God made the good spirits and Satan the human forms. It cannot be without significance that the Cathar discarnate entities saturated the woman, who acted as an intermediary between their world and ours, with references to St. Paul and above all to First Corinthians.* During the period of these revelations there were a hundred and sixty-five scriptural references. This points to Catharism having had its roots in Christianity. Certainly it was a totally different religion to what is now practised under this name but this is not to say that it does not derive from the teachings of Christ.

I do not think we need labour too much the undoubted linkage between Catharism and primitive Christianity. Surely the simple fact that the Parfaits main armoury was the Gospel according to St. John is sufficiently significant. That they used the Lord's Prayer is surely evidence, though its form was somewhat amended. 'Daily' was transformed to 'suprastantial' bread. There were also other amendments which have been lost to us. Nor was it used as commonly as it is today. It had an esoteric significance so far unelucidated and was not a commonplace repetition for everyday use for the croyants.

It may be difficult and even shocking for some to accept that the Christianity of Christ's own time, and of the two or three centuries following the crucifixion, was an episode in the his-

* See *We are One Another* (Neville Spearman 1974)

tory of Dualism. Conditioned as we are by sixteen centuries of Christian theocracy this is a hard matter for us. It must have been simple enough for the Gnostics and Neo-Platonists who proliferated in the first three or four centuries after the crucifixion. Here Dualism and Christianity are inextricably mixed with each other. It is also significant that in the recently recovered lost Gospels there are to be found more directly Dualist statements than can be discovered in the Gospels which have become the bedrock of Christianity.

The likeness between the practice of Catharism and Buddhism cannot fail to have attracted attention. Vegetarianism and non-violence are common to both. It must not be assumed from this that their philosophical and theological roots are necessarily the same. Much play has been made of the fact that the book *Barlaam and Josaphat*, impregnated with Buddhism and of far eastern origin, was translated into two or three languages before appearing in the Languedoc. Maurice Magre, a dévotee of Catharism, a plaque to whose memory is to be found near the summit of Montségur, described the Cathars as the Buddhists of Europe. This is a completely erroneous over-simplification. The philosophy of Catharism is quite distinct from that of Buddhism, something which could only be expected in view of its European and near-Eastern origin. Perhaps the most cardinal difference is that Catharism rejects the doctrine of karma, that we inevitably pay in one incarnation for the sins we have previously committed. The Cathars regarded such a doctrine as incompatible with the existence of a God of love.

It is interesting that Schmidt of Strasbourg, writing in 1849, mentioned that sometimes Cathar Parfaits were selected at birth. This is curiously analogous to the selection in childhood of Lamas in Tibet from boys who had been especially enlightened in previous incarnations. I am sure Schmidt's supposition was wrong because, in the selection of Parfaits, the Cathars leaned rather to those who had had experience of life as it is lived by the generality and who offered themselves for ordination at a mature age. It is nevertheless interesting to wonder how Schmidt stumbled on this idea.

105

CHAPTER FOURTEEN

The literature devoted to Catharism has increased enormously in the last three decades. In assessing its value one must reflect that a large number of books have been written from information filtered through the Inquisitors. This is inevitable because it is our most fundamental source. In assessing it one must allow for the fact that so much of the information from the Cathars was extracted under coercive interrogation and torture. Historians of international repute have taken as evidence against Catharism isolated statements wrung from desperate wretches stretched to the limits of human endurance. This kind of evidence has found its way into the text books and has been transmitted from generation to generation. Worse still is the tendency to rely on the writings of thirteenth century writers with a morbid hatred of Catharism. A commentator like Pierre de Vaulx Cernay cannot conceal his joy at the slaughter of Cathars and would nowadays be regarded as psychotic. He is quoted time and again as a reliable witness by reputable historians. In addition to his other shortcomings he had a depressing aptitude for describing self-contradictory manifestations of God's wisdom. If a stronghold in the Languedoc fell at the first assault of the Crusaders it was an example of divine grace. If the siege dragged on it was equally a manifestation of God's wisdom in allowing the benefits of salvation to be shared among a greater number. This man is accepted as a serious contributor to our knowledge of Cathar doctrine. One of his gems of theology which is still in circulation and often accepted is that the Cathars believed that nothing below the navel was sinful.

Another accepted contemporary source is the chronicle of Guillaume Pelhisson. It has been commented on by Duvernoy with his customary accuracy and calm. It contains the following interesting reflection on thirteenth century Toulouse. An old woman, a Cathar croyant, was lying in bed at the point of death. Someone informed her that the Bishop was coming to see her. She assumed this functionary to be a Cathar. A Catholic bishop learnt of her condition and also of her beliefs. He visited her, announced himself simply as the bishop and was accepted by the old lady as a Cathar. She expressed her beliefs to him and he had no difficulty in recognising them as heretical. He said to her, 'You are then a heretic because you have confessed your faith; know with certitude that these heresies are manifest and condemned. Abandon all that and believe according to the Roman Catholic Church.'* His blandishments failed and the old lady persisted in her heresy. Guillaume continues her story. 'The bishop then called immediately for a magistrate and many partisans of the cause of Jesus Christ (sic) and condemned this heretic. The magistrate had her taken immediately on the bed on which she was lying to the meadow du Comte and had her burnt there.' The chronicle then describes how the clerics were able to relax with a sense of duty done. 'This done (i.e. the old lady burnt) the bishop, the brothers and their companions went to the refectory and ate joyously what had been prepared, giving thanks to God and St. Dominic.'

What is so harmonious in this piece of writing is that the author's feelings are identified so closely, but without ostentation, with those of the rejoicing clerics. Guillaume Pelhisson is a stock reference for historians of Catharism.

The systematic vilification of Catharism since the thirteenth century has been as efficiently conducted as was its physical extermination. It is not surprising that in the succeeding centuries the literature, until the last three decades, has not been voluminous. English writers make two major errors depending on the period in which they live. The earlier authorities persist in regarding Catharism as a forerunner of Protestantism. This is based on the hundred per cent erroneous view that the Inquisition was established primarily to combat the Protestant heresy. This is simply untenable. No Protestant Church had, as its basic tenets, belief in reincarnation, in the creation of the world by Satan, and in the existence of forces of good and evil in

* Author's translation.

107

the universe from the beginning and persisting to the end. The errors of later writers are more those of lack of intuition. They persist in regarding the scientific and evolutionary philosophy of Catharism as repressive and pessimistic.

Peter Allix, writing in 1692, is interesting in that he recognises how for long before the advent of Catharism the south-west of France had been a centre of heresy. His book, *Remarks Upon the Ecclesiastical History of the Ancient Churches of the Albigenses* has two cardinal errors. It lumps the Cathars with the Vaudois who were certainly precursors of the Reformation. As a good Protestant Perrin exercises himself vainly in defending the Cathars against the horrible charge of being Manicheans. The similarity of the two faiths is undeniable. The Dualist interpretation of the scriptures is as far from both Catholicism and Protestantism as these two established faiths are from each other. A work produced in 1882 by Sir James Stephens, Professor of Modern History at Cambridge, is an especially deplorable example of a historian writing without intuition and with no critical capacity from the flotsam and jetsam of other historians similarly minded. The author's ignorance is almost total. He has no clue as to the distinctive nature of Cathar theology or philosophy. He obviously does not know the difference between Cathars and Vaudois. He says with hilarious insensitivity that the troubadour poetry is not worth preserving. He repeats the blind, pompous assumption of third-rate minds that civilisations necessarily die because they are decadent. He has no awareness that some perish because they are too advanced for the world they live in. He does not seem to know that history is written by the victors and that the latter are often liars. He says, 'The implications of irreligion, heresy and shameless debaucheries were probably not unfounded, if the word Albigensians be employed as synonymous with the words Provençaux or Languedocian.' Unfortunately even this assumption is incorrect. Albigensian is the name of a religious philosophy. The other names are used to distinguish the inhabitants of certain geographic regions. Perhaps for Sir James the south was inevitably associated with sin. For this author history is excitable and perjured journalism derived from unverified sources. It should be remembered that he held a chair at one of the most important universities in Europe.

Turberville does much better. He has no illusions about the low motives of the Crusade but sticks to the rigid tram lines of error in insisting that Catharism was a pessimistic religion and that, while the Parfaits were beyond reproach, Catharism was associated with certain aberrations. H. A. L. Fisher is reasonable and unprejudiced but refers little to the Cathars and describes them as Puritans. Of all past authorities writing in English Lea, with his *History of the Inquisition in the Middle Ages*, can be read with much profit. It has been argued that the Protestant bias of this American author is obvious, but is a Protestant expected to like the Inquisition?

Two works by contemporary authors are available in English. These are Sir Steven Runciman's *The Mediaeval Manichee*, and Zoë Oldenburg's *Massacre at Montségur* (translated from the French). The former is by a professional historian of international repute and the latter by a novelist with a sound knowledge of the broad issues of Catharism and the Albigensian wars. Sir Steven adheres to the view that Catharism was pessimistic and inclines to a no smoke without fire opinion of Cathar (croyant) morality, but his book gives a comprehensive view of Catharism and its background and origins. Miss Oldenburg is more favourably disposed to Catharism than Sir Steven but wastes some effort in searching for alibis for the Crusaders. A much neglected work is *The Holy Heretics* by Edmond Holmes, published by Watts in 1948. This intuitive but sober book expresses the spirit of Catharism better than any other book known to me in English.

Two works by French writers dealing with Catharism have been translated into English. One is Jacques Madaule's *The Albigensian Crusade*, which is primarily concerned with the question as to whether what was extinguished in the thirteenth century was a coherent Languedocian nationalism. He is as much interested in cultural and political issues as Catharism. Maurice Magre's *The Return of the Magi*, a translation of his *Magiciens et Illuminés* is not to be regarded as rigidly verifiable history but it is highly readable and traces the continuance of the esoteric tradition through the Cathars, Templars, Rosicrucians, Alchemists and others.

So far as French writers are concerned on the whole these avoid the cardinal British error of regarding Catharism as an early variety of Protestantism. Except for modern researchers they are equally obtuse as to its fundamental pessimism. What is most noticeable in studying French sources is the miniscule literature on the subject produced from the extermination of the Languedoc until the last century. Perhaps French historians have a sense of guilt about the means by which the equivalent of thirteen modern departments, comprising a culture and civilisation totally distinct from that of France, were added to the French crown. Of books in French published between the thirteenth and twentieth centuries undoubtedly the best is that of Charles Schmidt, Professor of History at the University of Strasbourg, who published his *Histoire et Doctrine de la Secte Cathare ou Albigeois*. It is competent, well-written and fair-minded. The author's protestantism does not obtrude. He does not regard the Cathars as out and out Manicheans but finds it difficult to regard them as primitive Christians. He seems to have been unaware of Catharism's great debt to the Bogomils.

Of other nineteenth century French writers Napoleon Peyrat merits being read. He was a Protestant pastor with a passionate and often romantic attachment to the Cathars. His *Histoire Générale des Albigeois* contains a good deal of fact and a certain amount of romantic embroidery. The tone of the book is that of an elegy. He adores the Albigeois, regards himself as the bard lamenting their slaughter and is at no pains to conceal his anti-Catholic bias. His book is highly readable, interesting, but not history.

Of modern writers Guiraud is in the first rank. His work *L'Histoire d'Inquisition au Moyen Age* was published in the nineteen thirties. Guiraud writes from the Catholic standpoint and starts off from the premise that Catharism was inevitably an error. He studied conscientiously but not always accurately the Inquisitorial records and assembles an impressive mass of information related to the theology, belief and habits of the Cathars.

The relative objectivity of Guiraud is offset by the bias and sometimes total ignorance of other French writers of the between wars period. When I began this chapter I took down from my shelves the only two books I possess on the general history of France. Both are by popular authors. How Bainville is to be regarded as a historian is a matter for the savants. He is certainly widely known in France and beyond it. In a book of five hundred and seventy-five pages, three paragraphs are devoted to the Albigeois. This modest contribution contains more inaccuracies and crudities than I can recall having seen in any other historical work. Bainville describes the Albigeois heresy as a political movement. There is no mention whatever of its philosophy, psychology or its religious activities. He says that one can recognise in it what appeared in Protestantism, a manifestation of the revolutionary spirit. It is clearly time that the worthy bourgeoisie of the northern countries analysed themselves a little more closely. He continues, 'They (the Albigeois) rose up against the ecclesiastic hierarchy and *against society*.'*
The latter statement is unsupported by any evidence. A number of anti-French writers hostile to Catharism base such views on what they believe to have been the Cathar attitude to marriage. Like the Quakers the Cathars rejected the judicial oath. This is sometimes used as evidence that they were enemies of society because the feudal system rested so much on vassalage sealed by an oath. But the feudal system had already begun to disintegrate in the Languedoc, in addition to which the simple fact that the ruling classes tolerated and contributed so largely to Catharism refutes totally the suggestion that the Cathars were anarchistic. Bainville's contribution achieves its apotheosis with the statement, 'The Crusade was preached across France as much in the name of order (law and order) as of faith.' But the integrity of France was not threatened. The heresy was principally on the estates of the Counts of Toulouse and Foix and of the Viscount of Carcassonne and Béziers. The Midi was emphatically not French. It was a separate civilisation with only a nominal vassalage to the House of Capet. Bainville is right when he says that, to the French, the enemy

* The italics are mine.

111

was as much the Count of Toulouse as the heresy. The domains of the dynasty of Toulouse offered an immensely rich and tempting prize.

Monsieur Bainville achieves a certain distinction in cramming a maximum of error into a minimum of space. André Maurois acquires merit by a totally different technique. He manages to write a history of France without mentioning the Albigeois at all. Some might argue that, strictly speaking, Monsieur Maurois is not a professional historian. I am not sure that the adjective necessarily confers a distinction. What is relevant to us is that he wrote three enormously popular histories of France, England and the U.S.A. and that, for better or worse, his influence was immense.

The work of the Catholic apologists for the Crusade is, for the most part, hollow and unconvincing. With the best will in the world it could hardly be otherwise. It is a little difficult in these days to justify the excesses of de Montfort and the Inquisition. A common practice of Catholic apologists is to base their case on a side issue and avoid hand to hand conflict on the main theme. Even a sober writer like Griffe builds his case principally on the fact that the nobility of the Languedoc were anti-clerical by preference and Cathars by accident. Even if we allow his thesis that anti-clericalism provided a suitable pabulum for the growth of heresy, this is no reason why he should pay such scant attention to the distinctive philosophy and theology of Catharism.

Another common anti-Cathar line is that the unity of France was jeopardised by the Cathars and that the campaign against the Albigeois was a necessary police operation. This is one of the main arguments of Belperron. It may be significant that he wrote under the Vichy régime, when Gaul was divided into two parts and its unity was a major and heartbreaking issue. Such attitudes exhibited towards the Crusade are immoral and untrue. France achieved its colonial expansion to the south as a result of the iniquitous Albigensian wars and the acts of appropriation by which they were terminated. Such a nationhood was not conceived of before 1209. Anybody who regards the Albigensian campaign as a kind of civil war must be naive

112

indeed or toxic with chauvinism.

In some writing of anti-Cathar tendency there is even the suggestion that the Meridional is an inferior being to the northern Frenchman, a consumer of garlic and olive oil and therefore in some way contaminated. There is a faint Hitlerian flavour in such writing. To be just, the dilution is inconsiderable but lends support to the statement made to this day in the Languedoc that Paris regards the Midi as a colony.

The accusations of obscenity and sexual perversion are, in modern French writing, less than one would expect, seeing to what extent these allegations are scattered throughout the mediaeval records. On the whole contemporary Catholic writers are fairly just and controlled on this issue.

In the last three decades France has produced what is, to date, incomparably the best available literature on Catharism. This is attributable in the main to Nelli, Duvernoy and Roché. Professor Nelli has immense gifts of exposition. He is concerned with the broad metaphysics of Catharism and not especially with its Christian origins. His knowledge of folklore embellishes and enriches all he writes. He combines an addiction to fact with a realisation of the necessity for intuition. Anyone wishing to know the basic features of Catharism should read his *Le Phenomène Cathare, Les Cathares,* and *La Vie Quotidienne des Cathares en Langeudoc au XIIIme Siècle.* Nelli was also responsible for the appearance of *Ecritures Cathares.* This is a vital contribution and the author's introduction is up to the standard of the book's main contents. Professor Nelli has also a worldwide reputation as an authority on the troubadours. *L'Erotique des Troubadours* is his largest and possibly most important work.

Duvernoy is primarily and supremely the historian. It is impossible not to admire his mole-like, unceasing and invariably accurate burrowings in the Inquisitional records. He has made immense contributions to our knowledge of Catharism. He does not claim to possess the *ésprit metaphysique.* One will find in his works no concession to intuition and very little to speculation. When he does allow himself to indulge in the latter he warns you with disarming conscientiousness that he is doing so.

113

Anything to be found in a work of Duvernoy is to be accepted as near fact as is possible in this world. It would be well if the professional historians, who have too often followed in each other's wake when writing of Catharism, could have availed themselves of the method, precision and conscientiousness of this Toulouse lawyer. Perhaps the most imposing work with which he has been associated is his edition of the Inquisitional registers of Jacques Fournier. His numerous short contributions, as to *Cahiers d'Etudes Cathares*, are unfailingly full of valuable information. He maintains always a continued high standard of accuracy and probity.

The third master is the venerable Déodat Roché. His concern is mainly with the transcendental philosophy and mystical aspects of Catharism. One of his favourite themes is the roots of Catharism in the works of Origen. He is the moving spirit behind the most important journal associated with Catharism, the *Cahiers d'Etudes Cathares*, and has made numerous contributions to it. His best known work is *L'Eglise Romaine et les Cathares Albigeois*. He is also concerned with the similarities between Catharism and modern anthroposophy. Monsieur Roché has, with unfortunate sensationalism, been described as the Pope of Catharism. No such functionary ever existed and, if he had, Monsieur Roché would be the last person in the world to aspire to such a title. Nobody claims that there is any official modern practice of Catharism but Monsieur Roché surely exemplifies, for this age, its spirit and devotion.

For those a little afraid of the mystical aspects of Catharism, it should be noted that two of its three great modern interpreters belong to the legal profession. Jean Duvernoy is a distinguished jurist and Déodat Roché an ex-judge. Another judge, Lequenne, also wrote a most interesting book eulogising Catharism. When one considers also the number of thirteenth century lawyers, including Pierre Autier, who were devoted to Catharism, it will be seen how much this mystical but logical faith owes to men whose profession is the elucidation of facts.

The three last-mentioned authorities will be remembered not only for the excellence of their individual contributions but

because of the impressive body of work which they have pro
duced. There are other individual works of merit. Söderberg's
La Réligion des Cathares is outstanding in its way. It is more for the
expert, a detailed exposition of Cathar theology in which it is
sometimes difficult to follow the main track through the jungle
of footnotes. It is translated from Swedish into French. *L'Epopée
Cathare*, by Michel Roquebert, is the first volume of what prom-
ises to be an encyclopaedic work and which takes the Cathar
tragedy as far as 1212. It is written with great clarity. The
author has submitted himself to the guidance of Monsieur
Duvernoy which, in itself, is a guarantee of accuracy and probity.

PART TWO

FOREWORD

In the preceding chapters I have dealt with Catharism as it is known to historians, theologians and philosophers. In this section of the book I am concerned with what has been revealed to me of its deeper teachings. These have been communicated by a group of discarnate entities. How I made contact with these is described in *We Are One Another* and *The Lake and the Castle*. Those chiefly concerned with my instruction were Guilhabert de Castres, Braïda de Montserver, Bertrand Marty, Pons Narbona and Hélis de Mazerolles. The first named was the most erudite Cathar Bishop who has not reincarnated since the thirteenth century. The others were alive in the twentieth century. Pons Narbona is referred to in the text as Graham because it is by this name that he is known in *The Lake and the Castle*. Hélis de Mazerolles is also given her contemporary name Betty because at the time these revelations were made to me I was more directly concerned with her than any of the others.

These communications are of great importance because of the light they throw on Dualism which is the oldest and least changed philosophy known to European man and dates at least from the cult of Demeter. As far as I know there is no hint elsewhere of their nature. Certainly I have not encountered any in the French and English sources or in other communications I have read from other countries. The origin of this information is, in a way, a guarantee of its unique nature.

I have dealt with what the revenants communicated under specific headings though often they dealt with more than one subject at a single session. Some topics, like that of creation, the nature of touch and the function of jewels were of particular importance to them.

119

CHAPTER FIFTEEN

The Transmigration of Souls

While reincarnation is one of the three basic tenets of Catharism the question of the transmigration of souls, that is to say the passage of the psyche from man to animal and vice versa, is an entirely different matter. All the revenants made it clear that we never reincarnate as animals. The idea that the cunning among us return as serpents and the ferocious as tigers is wholly fallacious. Such concepts are part of intellectually derived doctrines designed to make the Cosmos not only logical but over tidy. Once we have attained to the level of human individualised consciousness we can never reincarnate as animals or vegetables.

The reverse process whereby the psyche of animals reincarnate as men is undoubtedly true. I asked if it was possible for men to remember their incarnations as animals. Guilhabert de Castres said that this was theoretically true for a minority so infinitely small that, from the practical point of view, the answer was in the negative. I quoted the example, mentioned in a deposition made to the Inquisition, of the Cathar who claimed to remember the point at which he had dropped a shoe in his life as a horse. Guilhabert said that this was a peasant's embroidery, under pressure, of local folklore. In the Pyrenees to this day there are country folk who believe that we reincarnate as animals. A good deal of this stems from the rather degenerate and uncultivated Catharism which persisted in the upper Ariège at the end of the thirteenth century after the Albigensian wars were over. At this epoch the number of cultivated Parfaits was less than in earlier decades and some of the ordinary believers had become contaminated by superstition.

Guilhabert de Castres was very positive about the ascent of the psyche from the so-called lower forms of creation to man. I mentioned the emanation, sometimes expressed in the colours of the spectrum, I had seen on occasions round the petals of flowers. He said that this was the psyche of the flower and more specifically that aspect of the psyche which we would call the etheric body.

Guilhabert made the arresting and illuminating statement that all living things capable of sensation as we understand it are endowed with a psyche. By sensation he meant expressible in terms of the five senses of sight, hearing, touch, smell and taste. At first I assumed that, by this definition, he limited the possession of a psyche to the animal kingdom but it was made clear later that those plants possessing three of the five above-mentioned senses had at least a rudimentary psyche. There can be no doubt that plants respond to light. The germination of seeds is largely dependent on it. Many plants respond to touch and especially to those with green fingers, but we have more concrete evidence of this particular sensitivity. There are plants like sundew, venus flytrap and butterwort in which the response to touch is clearly purposive and the flower helps to engulf an insect or other nutriment or closes to avoid damage to itself. Less known but equally valid is the sensitivity of flowers to sound. Cut flowers of certain species wither at far greater speed than others if exposed to the vibration of an ordinary transistor turned up loud and left on for hours. Guilhabert reminded me that I had myself observed in my years of practice how flowers in the same hospital room would last far longer for certain patients than others. This was an example of the flower's capacity to pick up different varieties of human emanation.

The idea that there was a psyche in all living things which had the basic senses developed to a certain degree was a thrilling and revolutionary conception. What intrigued me was that the psyche was built in our rudimentary senses and, at its conception at any rate, not indebted to our more intellectual endowments. This was logical enough seeing that the psyche's most distinguishing feature is extrasensory perception which, after all, involves an extension of our capacity to perceive and can justifiably be regarded as an addition to our five senses. The logic of the latter standpoint is clearly revealed by the fact that we speak of the telepathic and the clairvoyant as being endowed with a sixth sense.

I was fascinated enough by these statements of Guilhabert but still more so by what he added later. He said that flowers, while being themselves incapable of appreciating perfume, were able, at their own level of consciousness, to appreciate the effect of their scent on men. It was for this reason that so many flowers had lost their perfume in recent decades. I remember years ago when the scent disappeared from the musk. I puzzled how this could have happened. Was it attributable to changes in climate, soil, habitat or was it some natural mutation, laid down as it were in the genes of the musk? I tried, in short, to explain this phenomenon from the standpoint of a laboratory scientist. What astounded me and what I could not explain was that the perfume was withdrawn from this flower in many countries and in different continents over a very limited period of time. This disposed of the idea that the loss of perfume could be due to local variations of soil and habitat. In discussing the matter with Guilhabert I saw that this loss of perfume was a demonstration on the part of the flower of a purposive intelligence. People no longer looked so much for perfume in flowers as they had done in previous centuries. This is especially the case in roses. Among the hybrid perpetuals and Bourbon roses which preceded the hybrid teas, scent was regarded as a basic necessity in the rose. This attitude was continued with the appearance of the first hybrid teas, diminished with their later development and is no longer maintained in the largely scentless floribundas. Many flowers have therefore withdrawn their perfume because its production is relatively superfluous. The scent of the flower is the means by which it seeks to attract the attention of man. It is also part of its aspiration to develop a soul.

The development of a soul and attracting the attention of man are two aspects of the same thing. When a flower is in full bloom it is speaking to us from the full range of its psyche. It is praying us to show towards it enough love to ensure its further expansion. Guilhabert asked me if I had noticed that many flowers with the strongest perfumes have the most inconspicuous flowers. In all the strongly aromatic shrubs like thyme, rosemary and lavender the flower was a subsidiary feature. Some plants express and develop their soul either through, on the one hand, form and colour and, on the other, perfume. There were all kinds of gradations between these two tendencies. The rose was regarded as the Queen of flowers because it had, in the past, beauty of perfume as well as form and colour.

The watershed in the development of a plant came when it was able to appreciate the presence of love and hate. This was the major step in its production of a soul. People with green fingers have a natural though sometimes unconscious love of plants and their success with them is notorious. At the same time it was noticeable that some plants thrived on neglect. They were watered and placed in what looked to be the right environment but failed altogether to flourish. Left in an unvisited room or disused hut they would take on a new lease of life. This was because the previous care given to the plant had not derived so much from love as from the wish to use it as an ornament. Under such circumstances taking the plant out of circulation could be a more loving gesture than watering it obsessionally each day.

At the same time some plants seem to thrive positively on dislike. In dealing with these one had to remember that plants could express not only the beauty but the evil of the world. There were certain growths in nature which looked evil and were evil. Some toadstools had a repulsive and malicious appearance. A number were in addition deadly poisonous. Some plants which thrive on neglect flourish because of the negative force of evil. A tendency to proliferate rapidly in the absence of nourishment could indicate, but not necessarily, that the plant thrived on maleficent vibrations, witness the fungi which grow prolifically on the stones of dank, underground cellars.

Speaking of modern roses Guilhabert said that the aniline dye colours so popular among modern roses was evidence that evil had inserted itself in the seeming innocence of horticulture. The harsh colours bred into the roses were a flamboyant challenge to reinforce their attractiveness to man. He pointed out that some of the most beautiful roses had originated without deliberate and planned hybridisation. The Bourbon roses which preceded the hybrid teas arose from a natural cross between China and Damask roses observed in Reunion Island. Roses like Stanwell Perpetual, beautiful in smell, form and colour, had originated as natural sports, the one specifically mentioned in a garden in Essex. Striving for a long flowering season in plants in which it was not natural was an expression of horticultural decadence. It was natural for China roses to flower throughout the summer. A few species of these had gone on doing so for decades. It was noticeable that some of the new hybrid teas and floribundas had a long flowering season each summer but the plants had to be replaced in five years, whereas there were Alba roses, like the old White Rose of York, still alive and flowering after decades.

Essentially the psyche in plants is limited to an etheric substance equivalent to the etheric body in humans. It is this which is visible when we recognize the emanations surrounding petals. It is only when the plant reaches to man in developing an arresting perfume, a perfectly harmonious form, or a capacity to heal that its psychic life moves from the primitive etheric to that of a more coherent psyche, making gestures, however subtle, to supplicate the attention of humans.

A plant cannot be said to have a personality structure in the strict sense of the word though some plants exhibit what looks like a willed intention. It is a gardening tradition that lily of the valley has tended to spread always towards the East. In my experience this is true. But though the plant lacks a basic personality structure it has the rudiments of a circulatory system. Its stem consists essentially of xylem and phloem. The latter expresses the channels through which the plant is nourished. The xylem is the structure by which they are supported. The phloem is analogous to the arteries and veins of the human body and the xylem to the connecting tissue which supports our arteries and our main viscera.

The revenants told me that the plant has also the rudiments of a nervous system. This is inevitable because a plant growing towards the light and a bud opening with the sun indicates the possession of a perceptive apparatus. The plant is especially perceptive in certain areas. The root system, through which it receives from the earth both nourishment and vibrations, is in some way analogous to the solar and sacral plexuses of the human body. There are also nodes at which branches leave the main stem which are especially sensitive areas responding to those other plexuses, like the brachial plexus, from which emerge the nerves responsible for the movements of our limbs.

I did not talk to the revenants of the exact mechanism of the leap taken by the psyche in its passage from the vegetable to the animal kingdom. They probably considered this beyond me. What was made clear from the outset was that the psyche of the animal survives death. That animals have psyches I had known from my own experience and have described elsewhere. That they survive death is another and still more important issue. The revenant who was Bertrand Marty in his Cathar incarnation and Mr. Mills in his life in the twentieth century told me that, in the zone of the after life in which he now existed, he quite often saw his old terrier to whom he had been very attached in this life. He made it quite clear that his contacts with his dog in the after life were not some outward psychogenic projection of an old affection because such psychological mechanisms said, often erroneously, to occur in this life, certainly have no place in life after death. The materialisation of the dog in the after life was as real as his own astral substance.

An animal with a developed psyche survives death and reincarnates in its own species except for the few who reincarnate as humans. A dog returns as a dog but the likelihood of its returning to the same particular breed is minimal. Millennia ago animals reincarnating could cross the frontiers from one species to another but this is unknown nowadays.

Guilhabert de Castres made it quite clear that the ripening of the animal's psyche, preparing its entry to man, does not follow in any way the pattern laid down in some of the accepted theories of evolution. Certainly he believed in the latter, though not in the Darwinian hypothesis which he described as lacking in subtlety. He emphasized that the leap from the animal to the human psyche was not achieved through the higher apes. The bridge was provided by those animals which had been longest domesticated, especially the dog and the cat. To make contact

125

with man it was necessary to form a psyche sufficiently mature to aspire to enter into matter as a human being. The dog had, of course, a primordial but by no means primitive psyche in its own right. This was revealed in the animal's capacity to pick up atmospheres in the presence of discarnate entities, good or bad. It was necessary for the animal to develop something like personality before its psyche became sufficiently mature to reincarnate in a human. From the theoretical point of view it might seem contradictory that the dog or cat had to develop the beginnings of personality in order to produce a mature psyche, because personality depends so much on intellectual pretentions and on the acquisitive and egocentric urges which make up the ego. Guilhabert pointed out that this objection was academic. Certainly the egocentric, timebound personality and timeless psyche were two different entities which were at war with each other in all human beings. This battle was an essential and inescapable feature of the human condition. How could a dog, aspiring to reincarnate as a human, do so unless its equipment included not merely a psyche but one which had gained experience in life in relation to personality, seeing that the harmonization of personality and psyche were an essential feature of the human state?

There is no doubt that many dogs come to resemble their owners in their quirks and personality traits. It is often very obvious that owners choose dogs which accommodate best to their personalities. Is it realised sufficiently that some dogs choose also their owners? The peculiar intensity seen sometimes in a dog's eyes reflects its longing not only for greater contact with a human being but the desire to become a human being.

It is noticeable that the domesticated dog is becoming liable to an increased range of diseases. There is a growing incidence of cancer and diabetes. Heart conditions like coronary disease are also increasingly common. The dog's destiny, in a natural state, was to suffer from infective and parasitic conditions and to die in age of different kinds of deterioration of the heart and blood vessels. With the development of personality he becomes more prone to those diseases which afflict human beings. A good deal of stress disease, coronary disease and cancer to which the human individual is prone are transmitted through the dog's psyche and expressed by his personality.

One of the acid tests which indicate an animal's readiness to make the next step in reincarnation as man is revealed by his capacity to use his psychic gifts to help his master or mistress. I knew a dog which could recognize that my wife and I were visiting his mistress when we were driving in a car and before we had turned the corner from the square to the street in which she lived. In the rush hour, when we were one of a stream of traffic, this animal, on the top floor of a high house, would raise the roof with his barks. He could also recognise the presence of discarnate entities. When a curse was laid on his mistress by a venomous paranoic, a monster of evil, he died of what was diagnosed as a virus infection, in my experience a notoriously common response to the force of evil. The revenants Braïda de Montserver, Bertrand Marty and Guilhabert de Castres all said that he absorbed the evil on behalf of his mistress and saved her life at the expense of his own. They indicated that a dog of this degree of development is not far off reincarnating as a human being.

Horses as well as cats, dogs and birds are able to reincarnate as humans. Though not a domesticated animal to the degree manifested by the dog and cat, horses have lived for hundreds of years in close proximity to man and reincarnate more readily than the higher apes, though not as frequently as dogs and cats because of their limited perceptivity. The horse does what its master wants him to do. A cat and a dog know what his master feels. The great point to be noted in this question of animals reincarnating in men is that the ape, though high in the scale of evolution according to the evolutionists, is low in the list of candidates for reincarnation as men. This is because so many of the higher apes have retained in full measure the aggressive impulses of the lower animals. This aggression may cease to be dramatically manifested and may be replaced by a cunning acquisitiveness combined with furtive aggression. It is the capacity of the dog and cat to live peacefully and passively with man which qualifies him for reincarnation in human form.

This pre-occupation with the different potential of animals to reincarnate as man should not blind us to the fact that most have coherent if primitive psyches. A chicken continues to walk after its head has been cut off because the psyche has not yet separated itself from the body.

Sometimes the vestiges of our previous existence as animals can be seen in the human face. There are women who in feature, form and gesture are genuinely feline. There are also what I have regularly called kitten men in whom feline attributes are often associated with great charm. I have noticed that such types inherit the natural and athletic elegance and competence of the cat tribe. I have remarked also that, with them, an appearance of polish and sophistication is sometimes accompanied by a remarkable shallowness in all which concerns the world of ideas. It is as though they have evolved with ease and polish in some ways but remarkably little in others. Guilhabert de Castres told me that the people whom I had categorized as kitten men were actually displaying in their features, movements and mental attitudes the characteristics of the cat tribe. There are people who look foxy because the fox is among their psychic ancestors. I also recognize what I call the bird tribe among people with little heads, small, sharp features and receding foreheads and chins. Guilhabert stressed that such people had an ornithological psychic ancestry. According to him the expression bird brain used of those endowed with a kind of twittering incompetence has a similar justification.

The cat is one of the best adapted bridges available to the animal kingdom in its aspiration towards a human psyche. Certainly the cat's love and loyalty can be to place rather than person and because of this he makes the leap from animal to human psyche less frequently than dogs. Nevertheless he still does so often enough. The cat's addiction to place is not geographically determined nor is it influenced, as is commonly believed, by his concern for his own comfort in the wordly sense of the word. The cat is more sensitive to atmospheres and to the discarnates who inhabit them than to human beings. His perception of these entities facilitates his passage to the more developed psyche of the human being. His development of personality is less evident than in the case of the dog which ensures that, when he does incarnate as man, he carries with him evidence, in relation to the dog, of a certain superficiality and impoverishment in the personality. Nevertheless his high capacity to perceive atmospheres in the presence of discarnates has led him in the past, particularly by the Egyptians, to be regarded as a sacred animal. In ancient Egypt he was often given a luxurious funeral like his master. The fact that he has little or no herd instinct also indicates at least the potentiality for a higher degree of psychic development. During and after the Middle Ages in Europe the cat was under a cloud and was regarded as the companion of the diabolic. As the latter term meant so often heretic this need not concern us much. The denigration of the cat at this time is often evidence both of inquisitorial paranoia and peasant superstition.

Reptiles never incarnate as men. They are never able to construct the necessary bridge of personality. Their inner development, apart from their basic biological characteristics, is wholly psychic. In their psychic life they are, in relative terms, an alternating and rigid medium for the transmission of good and evil. They never succeed in harmonizing the two. At the level of consciousness – that is to say of their consciousness – they function almost always as transmitters of evil. Nevertheless there resides in their etheric substance the power to heal but this is never consciously exercised as in the friendly gestures of which dogs, cats and less often birds are capable. Biologically speaking the reptile functions at the same teleological level as the plant. It is limited to its etheric substance and cannot develop the dimensions of a psyche. Poisonous plants are basically of the same nature as reptiles. They have achieved at some stage in their history the form and functions of snakes but have failed to fulfil and maintain the obligations imposed on them as animals as distinct from plants. In reverting to the vegetable kingdom they maintain the venom of the snake without its form and substance. They remain in close contact with the ground.

The psychic evolution from vegetable through animal to man is certain but the unit of psychic consciousness does not always last the pace. The plant may incarnate as a reptile lying, like itself, near to the earth. For a multitude of reasons it may return to the vegetable state. The bridge between animal and man is a point of no return. Once we have attained human consciousness we are launched either on a cycle of lives in this world, with periods of raised awareness between each separate life, or translated to higher zones of perception in which we either return to the earth as revenants or remain in the higher and wholly immaterial strata of consciousness.

Braïda and Bertrand Marty said that the ascent of the psyche from animals to man is celebrated in mythology. The story of Pasiphae who, by intercourse with a white bull gave rise to the Minotaur, illustrates a link in the chain between the animal and the human state. This story cannot be regarded as a meaningless perversion of morality. It is an allegorical reproduction of the ascent of the psyche from the animal to the human level.

I raised the question of those myths in which the central characters are regarded as products of the union of humans and Gods. The characters in question are often of heroic stature if male or semi-divine if female. Was this, I wondered, another ancestral memory of the psyche making a further step upwards from the level of the human to that of the demi-God? The revenants said that such legends could be allegories not founded on basic truths like that concerned with intercourse between humans and animals, but that more often than not the idea that the father of the hero was a God had been to some extent based on fact and had found its way into mythology because it represented the persistence of truth. It was possible for what we call the Gods and Goddesses to intervene in the lives of human sensitives. It was very important to define what the ancients had regarded as Gods and Goddesses. These were, for the most part, revenants still creatively concerned with the inhabitants of this world. A girl of unusual psychic gifts could be taken over by a female discarnate entity in the process of benign possession so that, in the act of love, the psyche of the discarnate entity was, unknown to her lover, directing the response of her body. Later this fact could be communicated to her or she could piece it together from her subsequent psychic experiences. It was usual in these circumstances for the woman concerned to be aware that she had taken part in an act of love which was not entirely carnal.

The product of any such unions were wise men and prophets. The phenomenon of the woman conceiving, under the direction of the Goddess, that is to say of a female discarnate entity, was the most important variety of these semi-psychic unions because it involved ultimately the worship of the Mother Goddess and because it emphasized the important role played by the earthly woman as mother of the great prophets. These semi-psychic unions were halfway to the concept of the virgin birth.

There was also the phenomenon of the human male being taken over by a male discarnate entity regarded as a God. This was better known but not necessarily more common. The result of such unions were heroes rather than prophets or healers. That the hero appeals more to the popular mind than the prophet explains why this form of psycho-physical union is more commonly recorded. In any case the myth of the child of the God or Goddess is well founded, provided that for Gods and Goddesses we substitute the terms discarnates or revenants.

What I have described in the foregoing paragraph involves the phenomenon of benign possession. The woman, or man as the case may be, is taken over for a creative purpose. Any child born of such unions is an exceptional being who the world needs at that particular hour. This is, indeed, planned birth on the celestial scale. It was always excessively rare and for this reason passed into mythology, but what we in modern times have read simply as legend is soundly based. This phenomena still occurs. It is rarer than ever because a rationalist civilisation and a till recently almost total abandonment of the idea that we are encompassed by discarnate entities, has reduced sensitivity to the degree that heroes and saviours of mankind can no longer be produced, except extremely rarely by the deliberate intention of those who watch over us.

It is curious that, while the fathering of heroes by the so-called Gods has always been true and has rarely been accepted in modern Europe, the idea that the Devil and his disciples could have intercourse with willing humans was implicity believed by many for centuries and was one of the charges

131

commonly levelled against witches. This particular myth is wholly without foundation. It was a product of paranoia on the part of the worst witch hunters and the mass hysteria of a superstitious and ignorant population. Conscious desire for intercourse on the part of the witch is a totally different proceeding from being the unknowing partner of someone already taken over by a benign entity. The question arises, is there an evil equivalent of the form of benign possession we have described as resulting in the birth of the heroic and exceptional? Intercourse with the Devil is a perverted and untenable fantasy. But can a woman sensitive be taken over by a dark entity and, by the co-operation of an unknowing man, produce a child? This can only happen if the woman is already depraved. The idea of a highly sensitive innocent being taken over in this way is beyond possibility. Cases of children being born as a result of evil possession are excessively rare. Evil is never a truly creative influence in any sphere, including that of the flesh.

CHAPTER SIXTEEN

Auras

In the early Autumn of 1973 Braïda de Montserver was talking a great deal about the nature of colour. A good deal of what she said was too complicated for a book of this nature but the information she gave me about auras was readily understandable. Every human being has an aura, that is to say a distinctive emanation of colours. These latter are only perceived by certain sensitives. The combination of colours varies with the individual. It is impossible to describe the different combinations because many colours are involved in each individual arrangement. In many people there is a dominant colour. Those who see auras are apt to describe individuals in terms of these dominant colours, of which green appears to be the most common. The description a 'green man' has nothing to do with being close to nature. It merely records the dominant colour of the person's aura. It is not inevitable that the individual should have a single predominant colour. Two or three colours may stand out among an infinity of minor variations. My own particular colours are blue and green.

The colours comprising the auras of those with psychic gifts are to be found from the green to the violet end of the spectrum. They begin at the extremity of the green band where it impinges on the blue.

The conception of the aura of the individual can, or could be, extremely useful in diagnosis because the colours change in disease. I was told that when I am exhausted the predominant colour of my aura is dark blue. The blue which normally contributes one of my two main colours becomes more concentrated and the green diminishes in space and intensity. The aura of the individual who has the highest range of psychic gifts of anyone I know is predominantly amethyst.

The aura is also affected by the prevailing mood. Depression

133

results in the intensification of the blue band, anger glows in the red end of the spectrum and joy in the yellow.

Psychiatric illness results in a shift of emphasis beyond the green end of the spectrum i.e. in the blue, indigo and violet sections. The band of green impinging on the blue is also involved. In physical disease the indigo and violet bands are chiefly affected. Functional illness, that is to say disease in which disturbances of physical function accompany disordered emotional states with increased tension, are usually signalled in the blue and green zones of the spectrum. Broadly speaking, disease is expressed by the green, blue, indigo and violet bands.

It is already accepted that the aura alters in disease. Until I heard it from one of the revenants I had never even considered that the aura could change in the process of healing. Graham said that out of the body healing is a function of the etheric body. The healer travels in this for perhaps thousands of miles to those destined for healing. While he traverses space he also goes off the map as far as his aura is concerned. The vibrations of the etheric body register 'somewhere beyond violet and before the red'. This means that they are not demonstrable in the spectrum. They are pulsating somewhere between its violet end and its red beginning.

The number of human beings who see auras is limited. They are inevitably those of psychic disposition but, generally speaking, their range of gifts is not especially wide. Those able to see discarnate entities are not liable to see auras. This is because in those with this latter gift perception is slanted in favour of colour rather than form. The capacity to see discarnates is accompanied by a perception of silver and gold and light rather than that of the primary colours or those of the solar spectrum. Just as colour is a fragmentation of light so the seeing of auras is a version of psychic perception. It is psychic activity at the almost physiological level and is manifested by those especially interested in the workings of the human body. A number of these are healers or potential healers but operating fairly exclusively with their hands and generally incapable of absent or out of the body healing or of cure by accepting the patient's symptoms. It was emphasised that auras are seen not with the eyes or with any of the sensory apparatus of the human body but with the psyche. Those capable of seeing auras resemble dowsers in that what seems to be an act of physical perception is often determined by purely psychic activity, as in the case of those water diviners who can locate underground springs or water courses from dowsing over a map and without leaving their homes.

The revenants told me that plants also have auras. The emanation seen at the margins of petals is the aura of the plant's primitive etheric body. The latter in plants, animals and humans is the entity which possesses the aura and the existence of which is revealed by it. The auras of trees and plants are much simpler than those of human beings and consist very often of single colours. Different trees and plants have different auras, involving infinitely varied expressions of the different colours of the solar spectrum.

A significant proportion of people are benefited by the aura of trees and plants. But because of man's separation from nature this is less than it was. This does not mean that we suffer our worst deprivation in being collected in towns rather than dispersed over the countryside, though this factor certainly plays a part. It is more that with increasing urbanisation we have become less prone to think and feel in terms of nature. The continuous and excessive intellectualisation of man is a toxic process through which he becomes less sensitive to aura and other psychic influences. We still meet people who realise, consciously or unconsciously, the beneficial effects of the aura of trees and plants. I myself recalled, when discussing this matter with the revenants, an old miner subject to brief and acute attacks of depression. When these were impending he wandered off from his village and sat under a particular roadside tree. At first the villagers tried to persuade him to return home but he steadfastly refused to do so and stayed for hours, insisting that he drew benefit from the tree and absolutely confident that it shortened his attacks. Oaks, larch and sycamore are more beneficial for psychiatric conditions than elms or poplars. Beeches and limes are helpful but not strikingly so.

A curious and fascinating fact is that the beneficent effect of the aura of trees and plants on human beings is enhanced by the proximity of water. This ties up with what Graham had told me about the special curative effect of harmonised vibrations of light, air, earth and water. He said that this harmony was especially emphasised in the evenings of Spring and early Summer at the summit of a little hill in close proximity to Bassenthwaite Lake in Cumberland. The reflection of light from water was quite often most potent, from the healing point of view, at twilight. If one has lived or worked in such a place in a previous incarnation the therapeutic effect is still powerful because a psyche with far memory is more sensitive to the vibrations of place than one without this gift.

CHAPTER SEVENTEEN

The Planets

The revenants were very explicit that there was life on other planets. They regarded it as an absurdity based on the egoism of man on this planet that anyone could think otherwise. They made it clear also that life on other planets was not confined to primitive forms. They were positive that in some of these other worlds there existed higher intelligences than our own. These more developed beings existed mostly in etheric form. It was indicated that on other habitable planets reproduction was not by sexual intercourse but by a variety of etheric activity. It was only in this world that man resorted to coitus to reproduce his kind.

The revenants said that at the moment there was clear evidence that higher intelligences from other planets were trying to make contact with us. It was not necessary to postulate the existence of flying saucers to make this contact credible. A significant and unidentified flying object certainly existed and could not be discarded as mass illusion. (The revenants were unhappy with the phrase mass illusion and asked if such a phenomenon could possibly exist. Mass delusion and mass hysteria were common enough but could a significant proportion of a rationalist population be persuaded to see what the greater number among them did not want to see?)

Contact with us was being attempted from other planets by the emission of vibrations of different wavelengths. Some of these were recordable scientifically but no one had an inkling as to their interpretation. That this communication from other planets was by means of vibration was inevitable because it only came from those inhabited by people of a higher intelligence and at a higher level of perception of awareness than ourselves. Such communication was necessarily psychic in nature and therefore vibrational. It represented what a minority of people can achieve a few times and for brief intervals on this earth. On the other planets psychic awareness can be maintained for a longer time at a higher level.

The existence on other planets of beings similar but mostly superior to human beings is inevitable because in the future we will reincarnate on other planets. Some are doing so already. This number will be greatly augmented in the future. This reincarnation on other planets is necessitated by the inevitable death of our own. I told the revenants I had been taken to task by some for indicating that I believed that the death of our planet was inevitable. The revenants said that such criticism showed an inability to realise or confront the facts of the Cosmos. It was not merely a question of our planet being doomed to a tragic and cataclysmic end by atomic warfare or by the unleashing of the forces of nature due to scientific man's insistence in handling material he is too immature to manipulate. That planets grow cold and die is and always has been a law of nature. The universe is littered with the wreck of dead stars. It is part of the unreason of man that the majority cannot accept the facts known to any serious astronomer. Furthermore other planets are built from the wreck of the old. This, too, is a law of nature, an example of the cosmic fact that in every death there is a rebirth. This applies from the simple plant dying back in Autumn to feed the earth with the wreckage of its leaves right up to the formation of new worlds from the wreck of the old.

After the destruction of this earth the reincarnation of people on other planets will depend on the degree of development they have attained on this. Those who in this world have learnt to transcend, however little, the limitations of matter will reincarnate in androgynous forms, that is to say in bodies with both male and female characteristics. This striking communication is not a new idea. It was foreshadowed in ancient Greece in those statues of the hero which show the male with female characteristics in the form of well developed breasts and a female distribution of tissue at the neighbourhood of the hips. (The Goddesses were never shown with male characteristics because the ancients recognized that the Mother Goddess was a truly primordial figure. The eternal feminine was recognised as the

138

mother of virtue. Civilisation and culture consisted in the impregnation of male aggression with the passivity and intuitive compassion of the female principal).

Less developed types will reincarnate in planets similar to our own and even on a new planet formed from the wreck of that in which we live at present. The argument that new planets take time to form does not apply. Psychic phenomena even on this earth are revealed as timeless in nature. Precognition, for example, involves the bypassing of chronological time. In travelling to the farthest stars and planets the time sense as we know it is abolished. We even experience this dislocation of time sense in this world in flying in jet aircraft. Many people are disorientated by flying over too great distances at too great speed, and some in so doing are taken back to their lives in previous incarnations by virtue of a gap in the curtain between two incarnations which is opened when space is being devoured at too great speed by fast aircraft. In addition there are areas in the Cosmos infinitely far from our own world and inhabited by psyches wholly freed from the dross of materialism and from any attachment to this earth. These are the planets which the more highly developed psyches previously incarnated in this world will inherit.

As well as planets in which human beings of our world will reincarnate in the future there are also those which, for thousands of years, psyches of human beings have visited after death. There are certain planets which represent the planes of consciousness we inevitably achieve to different degrees after death. This is not merely a symbolic representation. The psyche, escaped from matter, actually moves towards the planet best adapted to its system of vibration. The psyche's destination is also determined by the degree of emancipation it has achieved on earth. Psyches not destined to return to earth pass unceasingly onwards from planet to planet. They are drawn towards their goal by the system of vibrations predominating on each particular planet. The level of awareness of each of these new worlds is a function of its rhythm and amplitude of vibration.

Psyches destined to return to earth inhabit only a limited

number of planets. Then they return to earth past the stars. This is recalled sometimes by the human child in dreams and waking consciousness. The descent past the stars is a retracing of the track taken by the psyche after a previous death in its aspiring ascent towards the planets. In the future, when our planet has ceased to exist, the psyches will descend to whatever planet replaces earth.

Advanced life approximating to human existence is only possible on planets where there is water. A belt of humidity surrounding a planet is inadequate to ensure life of any tangible degree of consciousness. Without water a planet only produces organic life in the form of vegetation. The latter consists often of lichen and of cactus-like forms. It is inconceivable that man as we know him on earth will succeed in establishing himself in this life on a planet inhabited by creatures with perceptions and intelligences surpassing his own. The very superiority of the perceptions of such beings will prevent his landing. It is not in nature that its higher forms should tolerate the menace of destruction imposed by lower forms of existence devoted to aggressive self-aggrandisement. Such superior beings have means of defence not expressed in material terms.

The attempts at communication by vibrations made by other planets are not designed for their defence nor are they an invitation to the inhabitants of this planet to seek to colonise new worlds in the stellar system. They are designed to educate us as to the existence of other inhabited worlds in the hope that, by informing us of the infinite scope of the Cosmos, we ourselves may achieve a degree of culture enabling us to raise our level of civilisation a little.

Seen from outer space, to the discarnates the planet we inhabit emits no light. This is because it is surrounded by a zone impregnated by the force of evil. The symbolic equation of characters of darkness with evil is in fact justified.

Certain planets can communicate by vibrations other than those I have mentioned earlier. Vibrations of an amplitude conducive to disease can issue from dead or dying worlds. Some of the vague ill-defined diseases from which men suffer, such as virus infections, have their origin on other planets. The latter are those which are dead or dying of the evil engendered by the life which has existed or is still existing on them. It is interesting that men on this earth should be sometimes more susceptible to evil arising on another planet than to that originating on their own. This is because man acquires a certain immunity to the vibrations of evil arising on his own planet. Biological necessity ensures that we are endowed with a certain resistance to the more immediate and ubiquitous menaces by which we are surrounded. Man not only acquires but is born with a certain immunity to the evil of his own planet. This congenital immunity is compatible with his dual nature, in that he bears in his own heart the energies of evil and good.

While many planets die, as do all things in the Cosmos, as part of the process of birth, apotheosis, decline and decay there are nevertheless planets which are more directly responsible for their own end. There are those which have perished in cataclysms, which have, in fact, blown themselves up in a final and violent abuse of atomic science. The revelation by the revenants that other planets have destroyed themselves by pushing the button is no more surprising than the fact that they do not think this world will perish in like manner. They emphasized that the number of planets which have destroyed themselves in this way is less than those in which, for personal and tribal advantage, so-called science has blindly got out of hand and released energies and consuming radiations quickly so that forces in nature have been loosened and have, of themselves, destroyed their worlds. The revenants said that the planets which have not died from natural causes have for the most part been inhabited by men or by something approximating to them. They have passed away because a limited view of science had replaced a total wisdom, because their inhabitants had ceased to see as a whole and to know when to stop. The revenants reiterated to me the belief of Rabelais that knowledge without conscience is the work of the Devil. They added that our present usage of atomic energy and surgical violence, such as heart transplants, far exceeds what they regard as knowing when to stop.

141

CHAPTER EIGHTEEN

The Creation

Graham played a prolonged and important role in instructing me as to the creation. So did Braïda who, though not basically of philosophical disposition, had the gift of expressing truth in a lucid manner. In addition to these instructors Guilhabert de Castres appeared on several occasions when vitally philosophical issues were being discussed.

It was made plain at the outset that when they spoke of the creation the revenants were concerned only with the formation of this world. When they spoke of the creation of matter it was matter as we understand in here. According to them it was utterly profitless to hope to comprehend, while living on this planet, the creation of the universe which in point of fact was never created. In the beginning was the end and the end was in the beginning. The creation of the universe was a process occurring out of time and therefore strictly speaking not a process because the latter is concerned with duration. In thinking of the creation of the universe we must realise that the instant and eternity were one and the same thing because time did not, does not, cannot exist at the ultimate centre of being. We can, however, consider the creation of *this* world because it is subject to decline and decay as we are subject to decline and decay. We in it are victims of the fact of duration.

We should never think of the creation, either of this world or of the universe, in terms of beginning and end. All the time creation and destruction are proceeding together hand in hand. We see this in the decay of the cells in our body and in leaf fall in autumn. A truly cosmic view should perceive, at the same time, on the one hand the process of creation and, on the other, the deluge and the final conflagration. It is necessary to understand that there is a harmony between the creation and non-creation of the ever persisting universe. The deluge is the echo of the creation heard at the same time. It is like a sound reverberating from a fixed point and travelling back by the same route.

This world was created by light. Light existed beyond and apart from our planet. The radiations of light were endowed with a capacity to return to the ultimate source of being from which they originated. This rhythmic movement backwards as well as forwards is reflected in the birth of the human child and particularly in uterine inertia. There are rhythmic contractions of the womb which endeavour to expel the child into this world. There is often an antiperistaltic movement backwards which expresses the reluctance of the mother to give birth or that of the child to being born.

In the creation of the world light, from a central source, is confronted by the return of its own vibrations. It is as though light were faced with its own echo. This confrontation produces flame. Fire appears out of light as it does in this world when the rays of the sun are concentrated through a burning glass.

In the beginning as well as light there was the ether of space. The ether is primordial. It is the atmosphere outside the limits of the zone of air around the earth. This latter zone of air is not primordial but is a product of the creation of the earth. The ether is the air of space. As well as being the physical atmosphere of outer space it is the medium through which the psyche and the etheric body move. It is through it that the psyche becomes independent of space and time.

The flame produced by the collision of outgoing and returning light combined with the ether of space to produce a vapour which was disposed in two layers. At the upper level of contact the vapour condensed in due course into water. At the lower level the result was condensation to earth and minerals.

The creation was not to be regarded as an act of love. The idea of a good God taking joy in creation was untenable. It was as fallacious as speaking of beginnings and ends. We get nearer the truth if we spoke of a centre and periphery. We must conceive of the centre as a vibrational node at the heart of a circle. From this node all vibrations originated. Now while the general result of the turning back of light on itself was flame there was

143

also a throwing off of fragments of light at those points of impact at which the vibrations of light turned back on themselves.*

These fragments of light are the so-called aeons. Some of these particles of light return to oscillate round the central source of light from which they derive. This was expressed in allegorical terms by the Cathars and others who spoke of good spirits electing to stay in contact with the Father. Other particles of light strayed within the orbit of what was created as the result of the eruption of flame from light and its combination with the ether to form vapour from which the earth was ultimately condensed. This straying of the aeons within the orbit of the flame and vapour, in fact into the zone of imminent matter, is really what we call the Fall. It is referred to in the Scriptures in allegorical terms as the Fall of the Angels but is in fact the straying of the aeons from the central source. This is the scientific view of which the Fall of the Angels is a convenient allegory. This is theology expressed in terms of physics. (Perhaps we would be wiser in thinking of it as meta-physics deriving from physics). The Cathars and some of the Gnostics had a truly scientific attitude to life. To the Dualist, in reading accounts of the creation of the earth and the Fall of the Angels, the golden rule is to substitute angel by the word aeon.

Up to this stage in the creation of the world there is no positive good and evil. We are still within the sphere of the central vibrational node or, if you like, God or the ultimate source of being. The aeons continue to oscillate round this node and even those drawn to the flame and the vapour are not wholly separate from it.

I have said that it was from the low stratum of vapour produced by the encounter of flame and the ether that the earth and its minerals were created. The matter of the earth was at this stage formless and not divided into specific substances. Then came sound which was the second great experience later to be classified as a sensation. Seen from *the point of view of this*

* That light can turn back on itself would not have been acceptable half a century ago but Einstein has demonstrated that light can bend in its course. So many of the findings of modern physics are compatible with the emanatory views of creation.

144

world sound was the first great sensation. 'In the beginning was the Word'. For Word read 'Sound'. Though sound was the original impetus to the formation of the matter of which the earth is composed, the formless and specific substance which preceded matter as we know it was produced by the emanation of light turning back on itself. Sound is the explosive result of the meeting of flame and ether to produce vapour from which water and the raw material of our world were constituted.

At this stage we have therefore the five elements – the revenants called them eternals and distinguished them from chemical elements – of fire, ether, air, earth and water. The air is derived from the vapour encompassing what was destined to be the earth after the conflagration of the fire and the ether. Water resulted from the condensation of the upper layer of the vapour and the primordial substance of the earth is born in the condensation of the lower layer. The original sound or word ensured the creation of the particular chemical elements from which our world is made. The impact of the word or great sound caused the disintegration of the precursor of our world into separate atoms. What we regard as firm, unyielding, as reliably situated under our feet, is in fact violently alive though normally we are unaware of the vibrations of the indestructible energy which permeates our earth and the chemicals in it. This energy, infused in earth by the first great sound, is what the religious call the life of the spirit and the scientist by whatever phrase he uses to denote indestructible energy. What we have to realise is that spirit and what we call matter are intimately concerned with each other because both are impregnated by undying energy, which in its turn is sustained by eternal vibration. Spiritual experience is concerned with the revolution and movement of the smallest particles of matter. Without these immeasurably minute particles there would be no vibration, no energy and no life. Life is a mote caught in the sunbeam of vibration.

The disintegration of the primordial substance of the earth into atoms gives rise to animal and vegetable life. There is as yet no good and evil. There is no evil because forms capable of preying on each other have not yet been produced. But with the creation of atoms the aeons circulating farthest from the central

145

source of being, but till now not subjected to the magnetic pull of matter, are now exposed to the influence of the atoms created by the eruption of sound through the earth's primordial substance. This is the stage at which we begin to talk more positively of the Fall and of the corruption of the angels. It is thus that, speaking in the terms employed by the revenants, light, from the central source and still operating within the aeons, is drawn towards and surrenders to the darkness of matter. We can say that the light from the ultimate source remains at least potentially radiant in the darkness of matter. If we choose we can say rather that a particle of divinity remains always in the flesh. The revenants more scientific and philosophic approach expresses the realities of the question with greater precision.

After the first great primordial sound had split the formless substance of the earth into atoms, different combinations of the latter were formed into crystals by the effect of the planets. We still see an analogous effect in those chemical compounds which have a different form according to whether or no they were formed at the waxing or waning of the moon. A schema of this primitive massive crystallization may be seen in the glitter of the snow on high mountains and in the intricate pattern of frost on window panes.

All mineral matter is alive but in different degrees in different minerals. A more intense life is locked up in the interior of jewels and semi-precious stones. This is why jewels first came to be venerated. The mineral is to be regarded as a crystalline form which has become durable. The light it reflects reveals the life imprisoned in its substance.

Animal life including human life is produced by the effect on water of light refracted through precious and semi-precious stones particularly the latter. Amethyst and rose quartz were especially mentioned. I spoke with the revenants of the reflection of the sun on the sea at twilight on a sunny day, and of how there is a stage when the light and the setting sun falling on the water seems composed of innumerable circular silver coins which, seen closer, are not evenly circular but of different shapes. The revenants said that it was from a similar effect of light on water that crystals were formed. The more water present the more organic life, that is to say belonging to the vegetable and animal kingdom, was produced. This was first revealed in something like amœboid form. On the other hand the more light predominates the more additional crystals are produced which in turn are transferred into precious stones which, by their capacity to refract light on water, serve as a reinforcement of the life-creating force.

The light reflected through stained glass windows in certain cathedrals in the Middle Ages was often an attempt to reproduce this aspect of creation. The reflection of light through coloured glass was a reproduction of its transmission through jewels. It was this aspect of creation which especially preoccupied the Abbé Suger who was responsible for the construction and embellishment of the cathedral at St. Denis.

Different types of man had their origin in different stones. Each of us has a primitive precursor in which we first experienced the gift of consciousness. Each of us is influenced not only by the constellation of planets under which we are born but by that operating when our primitive precursor was being formed.

The whole aim of treating illnesses or giving strength by jewels, something to be described in the next chapter, is an attempt to take us back to our amœboid beginnings. The aim of modern psychoanalysis is to unlock the door on the unconscious. That of treatment by jewels and semi-precious stones was to recall, at a deep vibrational level, the beginnings of consciousness itself.

The particular colour refracted through the precious stones in order to form the primordial ancestor of our consciousness influences the colour of the aura of the fully developed man. As my stone was the amethyst my aura is at the violet end of the spectrum the situation predisposing both to psychic activity and to a lesser degree to depression.

The earliest forms in the vegetable kingdom were similar to the antecedents of animal life. These primitive vegetable forms were lichen-like growths, distinctly though not absolutely circular. They later developed a nucleus and spread by its fission, by the simple addition of adjacent cells. The form and the mode of propagation resembled that of the amœboid forms which

147

represent the beginnings of the animal kingdom.

Guilhabert de Castres and Graham said that the effect of jewels and semi-precious stones was not restricted to the immediate creation of life. Each had a distinct and characteristic emanation. Minerals with a slower amplitude of vibration affect the development of plants. Others stimulated more the growth of animal life. Some had a dual effect. Minerals containing iron affected both vegetable and animal life. This applied to this day. Iron preparations are both useful in anaemia and as general tonics. They are also employed to stimulate the growth of certain plants such as lime-resistent heathers and, where required, to change the colour of hydrangea petals.

Mineral substances have retained something of the power they had at the creation of the world. They can no longer create life but are themselves alive and with the capacity to emanate. Schiller's contention that God sleeps in the stone is literally true. Jewels and semi-precious stones are still able to emanate the vibrations of healing though only to a psychic minority. There are minerals with an enhanced power of emanation which, like radium in cancer, have the capacity to heal. But this power to heal is accompanied by grave hazards. In excessive dosage it can destroy tissue in x-ray burns. Worse still it can assume the capacity possessed by minerals in the creation of the world to stimulate growth. Radioactive elements like radium can produce as well as heal cancer. And what is cancer but the acquisition by the cells of certain organs of the capacity to reproduce themselves in excess and at abnormal speed? Radioactive elements like radium and uranium merely retain to a greater degree the capacity for creating life exhibited by jewels and semi-precious stones at the beginning of the world. The trouble is that the life created by these radioactive elements can be parasitic on our own.

The investigation by scientists of radioactivity in minerals has become a great evil. It is often argued that it is wicked to use atomic energy in warfare for the destruction of hundreds of thousands but laudable to use it as fuel in industry for what are described as creative purposes. Such reasoning is crude and dangerous. The point at issue is that such knowledge should

148

only be in the hands of, and investigated by, a minority of people with deep insight and of great probity. We have already long crossed the line beyond which investigation of what Graham and Guilhabert de Castres called the living rock should continue. Nowadays any individual with the appropriate academic qualifications can be turned loose in a physics laboratory and, in his turn, release the raw material of a variety of calamities. The revenants emphasized that the whole pattern of modern scientific culture favoured the production of evil and calamitous results. The secrets of science should never be investigated except by a small, developed minority for whom science was only one aspect of cosmic knowledge. Such a minority would know that there were truths of science to be revealed to the few but never to be exploited. It was indicated that man would ultimately destroy himself by his abuse of the secrets of nature. Destruction by an atomic war was not likely because, in spite of the horrors painted by the amateur prophets, the devastation caused would not be absolute and would not involve the total extinction of life. What was infinitely more probable was an increasing frequency of earthquakes, typhoons and cataclysmic floods caused by an artificial release by man of the life-creating energy locked up in minerals and particularly in those we describe as radioactive. This constant exploitation of energy by man would induce an uncontrollable chain reaction which would result in the destruction of this planet.

In speaking of aeons circulating far from the central source of being the revenants were to some extent returning to the views of the Gnostics. The latter were also concerned with the problem of evil and its introduction into the life of this planet. We cannot say that the straying of the aeons from the central source was evil. It was more a kind of fact of celestial physics. It was with the creation of the mineral world that the raw material of evil was introduced into this planet. It was only when the aeons came within the orbit of created matter that they succumbed to the vibrations emanating from it. The light from which they derived was obscured by the shadow of matter. At this stage we are at the beginnings of the symbolism of Light and Darkness as representative of Good and Evil. But essentially the birth of evil is associated with the concept of time which accompanied the creation of this world. What were originally the vibrations of light were adjusted to different amplitudes of vibration and the creation of different forms of matter. Duration and with it decline and decay are associated with the birth, growth, senescence and death of different forms in the animal and vegetable kingdom. Speaking at the most basic level what imparts the element of transience to our life is evil. A flower is not evil but all the more beautiful because it is transient. It is the transience which is diabolic and a tarnish on the flower's beauty. We cannot spend our lives bemoaning the fact that what we love does not endure. We can only accept this time and evil which taunt us with so much beauty and then rob us of it. It is necessary for us to see that what beauty we encounter in this world is merely the image of what we will meet in the worlds to come. Of course the creation of form is also a milestone in the introduction of evil into the world because form, like time, is transitory and is one of the major mechanisms by which transience is expressed.

The end of the world will involve a process analogous to its creation but operating in reverse. This is inevitable because all death is birth and all birth death. When we die in this world we are born to a higher degree of perception than we have known here. When we are born into this world we lose the higher perceptiveness possessed by our psyche before its descent into matter. The first steps in the creation were the turning back of light on itself and after this the eruption of flame and the combination of flame with the ether of space to produce vapour and ultimately water. Without water and flame there would have been no life. A planet lacking these two elements cannot create animal or vegetable life. The revenants spoke of water as permeating all things, from the smallest intersticies of human tissue to the hard rock of mountains. They spoke of it, in terms very similar to Taoism, as the weakest and most unresisting substance in the world and yet as remorseless and, in the long run, irresistible because it is ubiquitous and flows eternally.

Water arising out of flame was vital at the beginning of the world. At its end water would arise again out of flame but there

150

would be huge and widespread volcanic eruptions with burning lava and after these eruptions a return of the flood. The earth would perish, as it had been born, of flame and water.

The revenants explained the decline of the human body and its analogies with the death of this planet. Our tissues are liberally impregnated with water. In heart failure we are flooded with it and, in our dropsical condition, the fluid collects in the lower extremities and in the bases of the lungs and abdominal cavity. As they were together in the creation of the world so fire and water will come together again at its end. They have done so before in other phases of our history, when the fire of volcanic eruption has been accompanied by the pouring out of flaming lava and later by great tides which have engulfed huge tracts of the earth.

The revenants emphasised that I must myself decide how much of what they told me I recorded in print. I realised that to speak too much of the end of the world is to win for oneself the title of pessimist and worse, and that there is a case for not alienating people who can absorb the truth but only in small doses. But in speaking of the end of the world I am only dealing with what physicists, astronomers and others have positively anticipated for decades. I see no reason why I should not make my contribution to a subject which these days is certainly brought to the attention of boys and girls of A and even O level standard. As a convinced Cathar I can only repeat the positively optimistic statement that on this planet we live at our lowest level of sensitivity, that here our sufferings are greatest and our joys most transitory and that we will reincarnate in other planets representing higher planes of consciousness. The revenants said that in the planets on which we subsequently reincarnate we will live more in our etheric substance. Such prospects are only depressing to those congealed in the strawberries and cream heaven of the more comfortable forms of orthodoxy or in those of the newer cults which are based on wish fulfilment.

CHAPTER NINETEEN

Jewels

I learnt from the revenants that all life, wherever it occurred in the universe, was ordered and part of a plan. They rejected altogether the tragic view of people like Hardy that man is a helpless plaything of the Fates. They denied with equal conviction the insistence of so many scientists that the Cosmos is an indisciplined jungle where different species evolve at each others' expense. At the same time they allowed that such opinions were pardonable and to some degree inevitable because the average man could only observe the universe from its absolute periphery, the earth which we inhabit. He was restricted to a time-bound and fractional view of the Cosmos, to a glance at a limitless landscape through a narrow fissure. Our so-called intellectual leaders were specialists whose views on the Cosmos were determined by the current attitudes of their speciality, be it biochemistry, biology, electronics, philosophy or art. Their influence was to narrow still further the field of vision of common man.

That the Cosmos was a divine and ordered conception could only be understood by men with a whole view of the whole universe. But individuals like Goethe and Paracelsus did not appear in every age. There were whole generations when no such witnesses were available for the enlightenment of mankind. Normally men had to wait until death for a comprehensive view of the Cosmos. After death we look, through zones of greater awareness than the earth, towards the ultimate strata where truth is comprehensible. A view of the truth was afforded after death to the many and in life to a tiny minority scattered over generations. It was only because the hour was crucial and that civilization was threatened that I myself was being instructed in these matters. Even in this world it was possible to peer through the meshes of time and to realise that the concept of

152

Cosmos and order was truly the opposite of the world and chaos. There was in the universe a directing intelligence. The same influence which made a hedgerow plant reach towards the light governed the movements of the stars in their courses. The revenants discussed especially with me the underlying unity of nature. We spoke of what was well known to me, of chemical substances the crystals of which assumed different shapes according to whether crystallization occurs at the waxing or the waning of the moon. The radiations of the latter affected not only the tides of the ocean and the moods of epileptics and schizophrenics but also the formation of crystals. Why was it that there were different jewels corresponding to different signs of the zodiac? The explanation is that, in the process of creation, the different minerals of which jewels and semiprecious stones are composed crystallised in different months. This was determined by the influence of the planets each of the constellations of which has a period during which it is emanating most powerfully in relation to the earth. This period of maximum radiation depends on the position of the constellation in space. The creation of the world and its mineral substances depended among other things on a harmonisation of the vibrations of time and space. This is celebrated in religion and mythology. The Scriptures, drawing primarily from Hebraic sources, say that God created the world in seven days. This is important because it introduces the concept of time into creation. The latter is not a statement obvious to the point of banality. The creation of matter essentially involves the intrusion of time into consciousness. The element of duration comes between the world of no matter and that of matter.

The preoccupation with the signs of the zodiac and the months of the year arises more from non-Hebraic sources such as the Chaldeans who were concerned with the influence on creation of the constellations stretched in patterns across the sky. This induces the concept of space into the process of creation. The creation of the world involved the merging of the vibrations of time and space. This aspect of creation was reechoed in the birth of Christ, when the Wise Men of the East set off for Bethlehem when the planets were arranged in the right order in space and at the right time.

Just as different jewels crystallise in different months under the influence of the stars so people are conceived under the same influence. We can also be said to be born, as distinct from conceived, under the same influence because the period of pregnancy is the same for all humans with small variations. Certain jewels are associated with births at different times of the year. We allude to birth rather than conception because the date of the former can be fixed with greater accuracy. It should be made clear that the influence of the planets at birth is inevitably different from that exercised at conception because of their changed position in the sky but modern man has ceased to concern himself with the influence of the constellations at conception.

It has been a source of wonder to many that for millenia man, and particularly woman, has valued inordinately and been prepared to pay seemingly ridiculous prices for jewels and semi-precious stones. It is quite impossible to regard this as a mass delusion or compulsion continued down the ages as an obsessive tradition. Mass delusions are not transmissible in this way. It would be odd if they were because each age has its own particular delusional ideas. Men treasure certain jewels because these were at one time of value to them. It is not in the nature of such a greedy animal as man to dissipate his substance on an unfounded myth. At one time, when we lived closer to nature and were more aware of immaterial presences around us, we were more susceptible to the emanations of jewels and particularly to those associated with our birth and conception. The lists of precious stones, regarded as standard by the astrologers of our own day, derives directly from earlier ages and older wisdom when these stones had a definitely beneficial effect on the health of the individuals who wore them. In our day such stones are not useful except for the highly psychic and to those in whom disease is associated with the repression of psychic faculties.

The idea that some jewels can act as lucky charms is, and always was, unfounded, though they have been worn for this purpose from time immemorial. At the same time some jewels can definitely be unlucky. By this I mean any individual jewel and not a type of jewel. Some people refuse to wear opals or emeralds. This is because in the distant past both these stones were regarded as especially beneficial not only to the health but in the philosophical sphere. The opal was the symbol for enlightenment and the emerald for truth. Individual opals and emeralds were much sought after as amulets and lucky charms. They were regarded by their owners with so much egocentric veneration that hostile vibrations were made to circulate around them so that in time they became transmitters of evil and, as such, bringers of ill fortune. By a supreme irony what was regarded hopefully and as a good luck token became in fact an agent of evil and misfortune.

The revenants returned to the theme of how the same tendencies and impulsions repeated themselves at different levels of the Cosmos. Man himself was a reflection in microcosm of the macrocosm of the universe. We had spoken of the usefulness to man of jewels. Did I realise that there were different areas of the body associated with the activity of different jewels? The diamond was related to the functions of the forebrain and in particular of the pineal gland the point at which, according to the ancients, the soul entered the body. It was the jewel of choice of a small minority who are able to achieve psychic communication through the activity of the brain. (It should be understood that the revenants were not referring to psychological communication by the aid of which we contact our fellows through ideas and sentiments, or to the biological activities directed by the brain including such basic acquisitions as the perception of sensations or the instigation of the movement of the limbs). The diamond was essentially the amplifier of telepathy, clairvoyance, precognition and, in rare cases, of healing on the spiritual level. Graham asked me if I remembered how Betty had on rare occasions worn a diamond in the centre of her forehead during the Roman incarnation.

The emerald was associated with psychic communication induced through the solar plexus. This form of communication is commoner than the cerebral variety. For this reason the emerald was in the past worn more often than the diamond. It was usually carried at the end of a long pendant so that it rested as near to the solar plexus as possible. Most precious and semi-precious stones are best worn in this position. I myself recall that, without exception, all the jewels I received from Betty in my Roman incarnation were suspended from pendants.

I asked Graham what exactly he meant by jewels being associated with the two greatest psychic exchanges of the body, that is to say the brain and the solar plexus. He said that there could be no doubt that in past ages, and in particular in our Cathar and Roman incarnations, they had been of definite value in two ways. Firstly they enhanced the particular gifts with which they were associated. The diamond worn on the forehead could increase the efficiency of the 'cerebral' clairvoyant. Secondly, it acted as both a sedative and a tonic to the nervous system. The point of primary importance was to recognise that the diamond and the emerald only acted on systems as distinct from individual organs. The system in the case of the diamond was the brain and central nervous system. It was quite useless to attempt to benefit say, diseases of the lungs and liver by the use of these jewels. They could still, even in this age, be of use to psychic individuals handicapped in certain ways. I mentioned a psychic woman with what is called vaso-motor disturbance. She is very sensitive to small changes of temperature and finds insufferably hot atmospheres which many others would regard as only reasonably warm. In adolescence and in her adult life she was subject to attacks of fainting from such causes and was always a bad car traveller. Graham recommended that she wear a crystal pendant. Crystal is apparently in these matters an efficient substitute for a diamond. The emanations it emits are very similar if less powerful.

The emerald influences chiefly the autonomic nervous system, that is to say the nerve supply to the heart, blood vessels, internal organs and the endocrine and sweat glands. It is therefore concerned with the expression of different emotions through the heart and blood vessels, as when our pulse beats more rapidly from excitement, and, through the internal organs, as when we vomit or sweat with fright.

There is a third stone which exercises an effect on a system rather than an individual organ or organs. This is the ruby which is related to the cardiovascular system which includes heart and blood vessels. Graham said that the ruby was helpful not only to those with disease of the heart and blood vessels but to patients suffering from blood conditions. It was significant that he said that a woman known to me should wear a ruby pendant. It was significant that this woman later developed leukaemia, the deadliest of all blood diseases, from which she made a recovery not attributable to the resources of orthodox medicine. The ruby differed from the diamond and the emerald in that it need not be worn as a pendant. This was because the circulation of the blood ensured that the effect of the emanations of the ruby were diffused rapidly through the circulation.

While dealing with the question of jewels Graham broke off to speak of the use of silver. Like the diamond and the emerald this metal acted on the central nervous system. It was especially useful in psychiatric conditions with a strong obsessional element. This was certainly proved in the case of a woman with severe obsessions about her small, easily managed house catching fire and who was taking up to half an hour to leave it in the morning when going to work. After three or four weeks the reduction in both her tension and obsessional rituals was quite remarkable.

The use of jewels associated with the time of birth, and of diamonds and emeralds as stimulants of our brain and solar plexus, is certainly in these days less efficacious than the use of the particular stone in which the precursor of one's individualised consciousness first arose and which I have mentioned in the chapter on creation. The use of one's ancestral stone gives rise to a phenomena not encountered in the two methods of the utilisation of jewels which I have just discussed. One can feel the activity generated by the ancestral stone within minutes or even seconds of touching it. The arterial pulsation induced in me by a piece of rock amethyst charged up for me by a strongly psychic woman was unmistakeable. So was the added physical strength and mental energy which I gained from it in a matter of minutes.

A fourth use of jewels is to dispel depression induced by

157

certain seasons. The people we are especially concerned with are those afflicted by the actual process of the light withdrawing in autumn. These people suffer especially in October and November. The second group are those affected by the established darkness of December and January. Those who miss the light fading in autumn and who develop depressive illnesses at this time are advised to wear amber, cornelians or moss agates. These stones reflect the same light and colour radiations as autumn leaves. Wearing them is, in fact, an attempt to prolong the gold of autumn and to shorten the winter for the patient. Those who become depressed in December and January need not merely the intensification of autumn colours but the restoration of the sun of Summer. This is best achieved by wearing topaz, especially the rather deep-toned varieties which reflect the mid-Summer sun. Citrines are sometimes as efficacious as topaz.

There are two other stones useful in depressions occurring at any season. These are the individual's particular stone in which his ancestral consciousness was first manifested. For me the stone in question is the amethyst and I was advised, in times of depression or exhaustion to hold the stone in my hands for a quarter of an hour daily. The other stone is the emerald, which is useful in depression at all seasons and in varied types of patients because green is the colour of life in being predominant in nature and its effect is to smooth out the irregular and hostile vibrations present in depression.

What I have recorded about the functions of jewels is not mythological. I have been careful to pinpoint legendary attitudes which have developed over the centuries when man still retained his love of jewels but became progressively ignorant of their true function. The curative properties of jewels was still recognised later than the Middle Ages. Pounded jewels were among the ingredients of certain prescriptions. They were not efficacious because the chosen route – they were swallowed in draughts of medicine – rendered them inoperative. Jewels exercised their effect by emanation. They cannot exert their influence by traversing digestive tissue. In addition they are not designed to treat separate diseases or isolated organs but to act on the great systems of the body.

In the present age the therapeutic use of jewels and semi-precious stones is very limited. It can only be operative on a negligible number of highly psychic individuals. In the course of the last three or four centuries, and especially in the last two, man has developed his intellectual at the expense of his perceptive faculties to the degree that he has become impervious to the emanations of jewels. The number of people sensitive to such radiations was greater in certain previous civilisations as in ancient Greece and Egypt and during the Cathar epoch. As man's outlook to life became more determined by this earth he became more susceptible to what he could absorb through his digestive tract.

Apart from the therapeutic effect of precious and semi-precious stones the latter have for centuries been regarded as symbolising certain qualities. The amethyst represents a search for truth, the emerald the attainment of truth and the sapphire the gift of healing. People with these tendencies very strongly developed often prefer to wear these stones, but this is a matter of the instinctive and intuitive recognition of the meaning of a symbol and does not imply that the wearers are aided in any way in their search for truth or in the exercise of the art of healing.

Reverting to the maintenance of different patterns of different strata of development Graham said that as well as the planets being related to the formation and the function of jewels there were also certain flowers which had exercised the same effect as jewels in periods when man's psychic development was at a higher level than at present. The lily was equated with the diamond. Their emanations were similar but of different intensity. The influence of the jewel was stronger than the flower because of its long ancestry and its less transitory nature. The effects produced by the lotus were the same as those emitted by the opal. (Both the flower and the jewel symbolised enlightenment). The violet was on the same wavelength as the amethyst. The rose was equated with the ruby. I was particularly interested in the latter statement because this implied that the original prototype of the rose was red. Opinion among the horticulturists has been divided as to whether the original European rose was red or white. Generally speaking opinion was in favour of the latter. It appeared from what the revenants said that the remotest ancestor of our modern galaxy of roses was red and allied to what is now called Rosa Gallica, known sometimes as the Apothecary's Rose. The rose was, like the ruby, a stimulator of the heart and circulation. It was formerly given for a great diversity of conditions. By the time I was a medical student it was reduced to being used, in the form of a liquid base called Aqua Rosæ, as a medium in which to incorporate other ingredients. The original rose was not as intense as the Apothecary's rose and was probably a deep pink.

The jewel-plant relationship was important because treatment by jewels in some civilisations predated the use of plants. The use of jewels diminished because man became less permeable to their emanations and also because plants were more accessible to ordinary people than jewels. It should be understood, in speaking of flowers, that one is referring to their emanatory capacity and not to their clinical constitution. There is, for instance, no evidence that the rose produces any chemical useful in heart disease. Digitalis, obtained from the foxglove, indubitably produces an agent digitalin which is still a sheet anchor in dealing with heart conditions. There is, however, no evidence whatever that the foxglove in its radiations has a favourable effect on the human heart. The beneficial effect of colours in nature is not limited to that of the golden leaves in autumn. As we have said the latter serve to prolong to those sensitive to their disappearance the light of autumn. It is for the same reason that among the Winter and early Spring flowers there is a predominance of those with golden and yellow tones, for example winter jasmine and later the daffodil, golden crocus, forsythia etc. The perception of the colours of the sun is beneficial to those liable to be depressed at this time of year.

There are also many white flowers in winter, such as winter cherry, vibernam fragrans and the snowdrop. The positively curative effect of these was modest but they are useful in symbolising the purity of the earth preparing for spring in its winter sleep. The predominance of the gold and white combination in winter and early spring flowers was celebrated in the earliest roses used in symbolic designs. These had white petals with golden stamens.

The intensely sweet smell of some winter flowers, like winter sweet, vibernam fragrans and some earlier daphnes, revealed how some of the more inconspicuous flowers called to man in the dark months of the year by the potency of their perfumes which revealed the soul of the plant in action. This was as much an attempt on the part of the plant's psyche to call to man as that manifested by the highly scented aromatic shrubs like lavender and rosemary which flower in summer but which speak to us more through perfume than conspicuous blooms.

Most of us have a favourite flower. In addition we have one which, in muted tones, vibrates on the same wavelength as ourselves. Our favourite flower and that which best represents our individuality are not necessarily the same. It is remarkable, however how often the two coincide. I understand that the rose is the flower on my wavelength. It is undoubted that I prefer it to all other flowers. One's representative flower can change concomitantly with one's inner evolution. In time past my favourite and representative flower was the violet. Generally speaking the more psychic the person the more the favourite and the representative flowers coincide.

The colour of the flower which best represents our individuality is by no means the same as that of the jewel which represents our most prominent and productive tendency. Graham pointed out that one of our reincarnated Cathars with a tremendous gift of healing is represented by a deep blue sapphire in jewels and by the daffodil in flowers.

Guilhabert de Castres added an interesting and practical item about the rose. Sometimes the thirteenth century troubadours sang ordinary love songs as well as those with hidden meanings. The former were necessary as a disguise for the latter. When the troubadours sang a song with an esoteric significance they carried a rose in their hands. This was a specialised continuation of the Roman tradition that what was said sub rosa, that is to say after a chaplet of roses had been placed on the head at a banquet, was to be regarded as confidential.

The need for a sign like the rose was greater in the age of persecution in which so many of the troubadours lived. The rose in question was like what nowadays the specialists call the Rose of Provins. The species commonly used by the troubadours was a small red bloom belonging to this family.

CHAPTER TWENTY

Touch

The importance of touch had been stressed many times by the revenants but it was only in the autumn of 1973 that it became a major issue. Graham emphasised that touch was a dominant among the sensations, that it was infinitely more varied and complex than colour and sound. Some months previously I would have rejected this completely. To me vision has always been the most subtle of all sensations. If I had been asked a few years ago my opinion of touch I would have said that it was the crudest of all sensory experiences and the lowest from the spiritual point of view. I was reminded that I had had some of the most remarkable experiences of my life through the medium of touch. Was not my first contact with the revenants engineered by touch? I had at first not been aware of their presence unless Miss Mills, the central figure in *We Are One Another* and *The Lake and the Castle* had touched my wrist or the base of my thumb. I was still dependent on such contacts when I understood for the first time what the revenants were saying and when I first saw their outlines. For many months, when Miss Mills' fingers were withdrawn, I ceased to feel, hear or see the revenants. When she touched me again my powers of perception were immediately restored. The effect was as sudden and unmistakable as that of a new battery on a run down radio. It was not until the revenants discussed it that I realised how completely physical touch had been responsible for my contact with beings from the next world.

Graham stressed that touch could activate the other senses to an unmistakable and dramatic degree. I had been aware of sweet perfumes, particularly that of cedarwood at the outset of the bouts of increased psychic activity which I experienced in the early 1960's. Graham now explained that this had occurred when I had been touched by Guilhabert de Castres. I mentioned elsewhere* the moving purple and dark green bands which a few years ago were for me the heralds of intense psychic activity. Now the revenants told me that these visions had been induced when I had been touched by either Guilhabert or Betty. The former could evoke, by touch, perfume as well as colour. Betty was restricted to the latter function.

The revenants clarified the issue for me. I accepted that touch could induce the perception of colour. I did not realise the enormous psychological significance of this phenomena. What it meant was that one sensation could induce another. I thought this only applied when I made contact with the revenants but they reminded me that the array of crosses and Dualist symbols I had seen glowing on the wall were induced by Miss Mills' touch and that they had faded when her hand was withdrawn. The same applied to the images of the rose, the chalice and the dove, an experience I have described in *The Lake and the Castle*. They said that what Miss Mills was transmitting by touch was a whole world of experience focussed on previous lives extending back to the Roman Empire. This was something more than ordinary tactile sensation.

Graham directed my attention again to the visions projected on the wall which I have described elsewhere. These visions were of objects of different shapes. This meant that touch could stimulate the creation and perception of form as well as colour.

Were there other sensations evocable by touch? He asked me if I remembered how years ago, in those weeks of increased psychic activity which I now know to have involved the presence of the revenants, I had had what I call hallucinations of taste as well as smell. At the time to which he referred I could feel in my mouth for hours a cloying sweetness as though I had been sucking saccharine tablets. At that time I was satisfied to classify this sensation under the heading of sensory migraine. I now learnt from the revenants that this was one more example of what happened when they had touched me.

Sometimes I had had a tingling sensation on the left side of the tongue. This very often accompanied the smell of cedarwood and the intensely sweet taste in my mouth. Sometimes

* In *The Cathars and Reincarnation*, Neville Spearman.

they came separately. I learnt again that this was another sequel of psychic touch.

I was told that the perception of both colour and form, taste and smell could all be evoked by the touch of either a highly psychic living person or a revenant. I asked, what of sound? I was told that touch could induce different harmonies but that this was a much rarer reaction. In 1954 I had suffered from Menière's syndrome. This had been ushered in by a rhythmic humming similar to the sounds I had heard in childhood and which later I had called the music of the spheres. I had realised previously to this particular conversation with Graham that the giddiness and excruciating noises in the head from which I suffered were attributable to my resistance to enlightenment. I had not understood until Graham specifically instructed me that in 1954 I had been actually touched by Guilhabert and this astral contact had initiated the rhythmic harmony which I had resisted and transformed into disease symptoms.

Graham pointed out that in all the so far mentioned manifestations induced by touch the effect had been to produce the timeless experience. I had seen the crosses and other symbols on the wall as I had seen them in previous incarnations. When I was touched by Betty the green and purple bands I saw were the colour of her favourite togas in her Roman incarnation.* It was emphasised to me that touch could also induce another simpler and less dramatic manifestation of being out of time. I had known two people capable of inducing in me, by touch, such a degree of self abandonment that I was unaware, at the height of the experience, as to what particular area was being touched or even if I were being touched at all. I myself had first had experience in the process of being massaged. Later it was induced by the laying on of hands. Others more sensitive were able, if they had shared previous incarnations, to pass out of time and be unaware of space merely by touching each others hands. Even a momentary touch by a highly developed person could produce in a sensitive an out of the body experience. I was asked if I remembered the woman who felt herself to be floating infinitely far above her body when being touched by a Tibetan

* See *The Lake and the Castle*, Neville Spearman.

165

lama. The touch of a great healer could induce a fusion of psyches so intense that, at this culmination, there was no distinction between healer and patient and no awareness of their separate personalities.

Graham reminded me that in the Cathar system of healing heat was felt in the skin and often in the subjacent tissues of the healer and the healed. There were two more sensations induced by touch in the process of healing. Very often arterial pulsation is felt in the hands of the healer and in the body of the patient at the point of contact. The hands and forearms of the healer may be shaken by a distinct tremor as he or she transmits the healing vibrations. Touch which produces such effects is not touch as described in the books of psychology and physiology. It is obvious that touch is not a single sensation but a group of varied sensory experiences. There are clearly different forms of touch. Some of these forms have the power to activate other sensations like sight, smell and taste. When I said that all this infringed the laws of physiology Graham said that the latter were produced by scientists who started by examining the individual sensation rather than by considering the Cosmic disturbance which activated the whole human organism.

It was stressed by Betty, Graham and Guilhabert that there comes a time in the evolution of the psychic individual when spontaneous touch, expressed in the form of an affectionate gesture, is equally or more potent than the conscious practice of any of the recommended systems of healing based on touch. We will all accept that love enhances the effect of touch. This is banal and self-evident but the revenants were not referring to the capacity of the beloved to sink in her lover's arms and obtain in so doing a joy which is too often transitory. Love, in the sense of the word in which the revenants use it, is psychic contact maintained through several generations. This is not a question of the individuals involved being consciously in love with each other. This latter condition can happen sooner or later in one or other of a string of incarnations and is always an impediment to psychic union. What the revenants mean by love is a unison of outlook which enables two people, even in this world, to present identical attitudes when confronted with the same phenomena.

Under such circumstances two people can think feel and talk in completely identical terms. Brief spontaneous touch between two such people can abolish quickly any physical symptoms from which they are suffering.

This very speedy abolition of symptoms can only occur between two people who are born psychic. A single highly psychic person can, however, remove some of the pains of even non-psychic individuals in a matter of minutes. Conditions like migraine and fibrositis can be cured in this way.

I then discussed with Graham how Christ healed by touch. Here we come to the heart of the matter. Christ could heal lepers and the blind by a single touch. He could raise the dead in an instant. Was this, I asked, merely a glorified extension of what happened when a psychic person took away a woman's fibrositis by touching her shoulder? I was now instructed that, broadly speaking, there were three kinds of touch. There was first touch as we understand it in this world and by which we appreciate the shape, density and temperature of objects. This was touch pure and simple, touch, as it were, limiting itself to what could normally be felt with our fingers. There was also the form of touch employed by the sensitive who, when holding my wrists or thumb, enabled me to see crosses and symbols from past reincarnations as well as endowing me with a capacity to feel the presence of and see and speak with the revenants. This was etheric touch. It was essentially a function of the psyche which, under the circumstances described was manifesting itself through the etheric body. The psyche used also the same vehicle of communication in out of the body healing in which the healer is transported in his or her etheric form hundreds or thousands of miles to relieve the afflicted.

Graham defined the third variety of tactile sensation as astral touch. It was, in fact, the name given to the process of being touched by the revenants. When I had, in 1954 and in the early 1960's, been touched by Guilhabert de Castres, dead about 1241, this was an example of astral touch. Graham was careful to point out that Betty had also touched me in the early 1960's and had induced the visions of the purple and green bands. Though she had produced the same visual effects as Guilhabert

167

the mechanism was different. She was using etheric touch because at that time she was still living on this planet.

There were other forms of astral touch more directly recognisable than that involved in the production of colours. The sensations I had experienced after being touched by the revenants came under this heading. I had felt a deep and penetrating heat after I had badly jarred my right hip and Graham himself, from the other world, had laid his hands upon the affected area. Astral touch was also responsible for the feathery and exhilarating coldness I felt just above rather than in my skin when Betty returned to me after her death in this life and laid her fingers upon me.

Etheric touch was essentially an attribute of the living. It was given to a proportion of those with psychic gifts. It was part of the basic equipment of those employed in psychic healing. It was to be noted that Betty had employed etheric touch in her life time and astral touch after her death.

Astral touch was essentially, but not always, an attribute of those who had left this world. It was responsible for the zone of coldness I had felt in being touched by the revenants. The latter sensation was as much a healing phenomenon as the deep and pulsating heat I had felt from contact with their fingers. Nevertheless there were rare beings who were capable of bestowing the benefits of astral touch even in this life. Christ could not have raised Lazarus from the dead or enabled the man blind from birth to see by etheric touch alone. Christ was able to use astral touch in his life because he was a special kind of being. The matter of which he was composed was so spiritualised that he could escape wholly from it even in this life. This is what happened when he appeared before his disciples invested in light at the Transfiguration on the Mount. The number of people in any generation capable of existing in their astral body even for what, in terms of clock time, would be a few moments, is negligible. Nevertheless such people do exist. They are in this world because they have a special message to transmit. The gifts they acquire by the capacity to exist in their astral bodies are essentially those which qualify them to carry the message with which they are entrusted. Such people were more numerous in the first two centuries after Christ. They were fed directly by his emanation. There was a significant increase in the number of people in the thirteenth century. The majority appeared as Cathars. After seven centuries, as an antidote to the engulfing materialism of the times, the proportion of people so gifted is rising again but can never be more than a drop in the ocean.

Graham then told me something which I found bewildering. He said that some people have the gift of bestowing on an inanimate object the power to stimulate psychic activity. This is *not* the same as psychometry, the art by which a sensitive can describe details from the present and past lives of individuals by handling objects belonging to them. Graham was speaking of the process of actively and deliberately charging an object so that it became endowed with the power to stimulate recall of past lives or to increase the healing power of any other sensitive holding it. This could be done by a person of exceptional psychic gifts handling a semi-precious stone like rose quartz or rock amethyst for a quarter of an hour a day for a few weeks. The stone could then be given to another sensitive who would not only find his powers of healing and recall to be enhanced but would find himself strengthened and restored by handling the stone for a few minutes.

I was astonished to find that this phenomenon was a manifestation of astral touch. It seemed to me inconceivable that a power conferred in this life on an inanimate object was of the same nature as that transmitted by the touch of the revenants. I could not imagine why such a phenomenon should be regarded as a higher level of activity than out of the body excursions conducted by the etheric body in the process of psychic healing. It was explained to me that a charged mineral of this nature was not expressing the functions of either the etheric or astral bodies. The etheric body could not, without damage to the individual, stay out of the body more than a limited period of time. The capacity of the astral body to detach itself from the individual *in this life* was so rare as to be almost negligible and was highly dangerous. What happened when a stone was charged in the way I have described was that a revenant touched, with his astral body, a highly developed living sensitive who, by holding a stone, set in motion, through her etheric body, a system of vibrations which harmonised with those imprisoned in the stone. The latter was induced to vibrate at a different rhythm than previously. This changed rhythm of vibrations enabled another sensitive to whom the stone was given to heighten his own powers of recall and healing. This deliberate and intentional charging of a stone in this life was excessively rare. It was a rush job not to be used light heartedly. That it was done at all was evidence of the darkness of the current spiritual climate. It was necessary to replenish the flagging resources of a minority of people needed for the transmission of the truth. But though this process was rare and, strictly speaking untraditional it stemmed from the practice, in highly spiritual communities, of a minority of initiates to wear emblems worn by specially enlightened predecessors. Guilhabert de Castres reminded me that I had received from him a miniature model of a dove which he himself had worn for years.

Any reasonable person would ask at this stage in what way this differs from the conservation of holy relics, like the bones or even nail parings of Saints, as practised in the Catholic and other Churches. It seemed to me that what was sauce for the goose was sauce for the gander and that the Cathars were merely continuing a practice which, in other faiths, has often been regarded as superstitious. The revenants were very emphatic that this was not the case. They said I should examine this question against the background of all they had said previously about the creation of the world and the life imprisoned in minerals. They pointed out that the objects which could be used in this way are ordinary minerals, including semi-precious stones and metals and that there was nothing intrinsically sacred about them. A metal dove was not sacred because Guilhabert de Castres had worn it. It was, however, more useful because he had reinforced it with his own vibrations. This was the diametric opposite of conserving the bones and mummified bodies of so-called Saints. To offer reverence to such relics was to personalise religion and corrupt its nature. The use of charged stones and medallions worn by the

170

enlightened was essentially scientific in the broadest sense of the term. Its aim was always to heighten the psychic potentialities of the individual. Where an object had previously been worn by a highly developed predecessor it was not to be regarded as a target for reverence but as something of proved value, like a well with healing properties or an especially beneficent and well sited centre of healing. In considering this question we were, in fact, dealing with a basic medical issue. The more psychic the individual the more he will respond to the vibrations of minerals and metals. The less psychic the more he depends on the ingestion of chemical compounds in the form of pills, capsules and liquid medicines.

The revenants mentioned everyday factors which affected the efficiency of touch. With some individuals there is a daily variation in the capacity to respond to either corporeal, etheric or astral touch. In some perception is relatively blunt in the morning and increases in the evening. In others the reverse is true. In some it is influenced by place as well as time. There are certain sites with a strong emanatory capacity which for this reason have become holy places and where the effect of touch is considerably enhanced. It is still further fortified if the sensitive has some association with a place in a previous incarnation. For many sensitives psychic contact in the past is a far more potent influence than the general emanatory capacity of any particular site. There are so-called holy places which have no effect on me at all and enhance none of my perceptions including that of touch.

Exhaustion may blunt the perception of touch and reduce its effects but this is by no means inevitable. Different individuals vary enormously in this particular. Sometime exhaustion acts like acute illness in enhancing the perception of touch. It does so by facilitating the separation of the psyche from the personality so that the effects of the more refined forms of touch are amplified.

Graham returned to the theme of ordinary human affection in relation to touch. He reminded me how Betty had stimulated in me the perception of the dark green and purple bands. He said she had done this by the power of recall and affection. Her

171

psyche was, at this time, engaged in a two-way mechanism. It was partly tuned in to the thirteenth century when she and I, sister and brother, had been very fond of each other. The recall of our mutual affection seven centuries previously had stimulated her, below the conscious level, to reach out towards me, in the twentieth century, in an out of the body experience. This had resulted in her touching me with her etheric fingers.

Graham spoke also of sex in terms of touch and as a passport to self abandonment. He agreed that it afforded the average sensuous individual his or her most likely opportunity for self forgetfulness. There was a little death at the heart of every fully executed physical act of love as distinct from the mere satisfaction of a physical appetite. It signified to common man that the ultimate goal of sensation is its own death. What was an orgasm but an intense accumulation of sensation exploding in a kind of blankness of no-sensation? The latter is more intense than the sensory experience leading up to it. It is, in a way, a kind of new perception. The trouble is that the latter is momentary. It does not become an endowment. It depends on the physical caprices of two people whose capacity for this experience becomes blunted with time. Seen in this life the sex act is a brief and dramatised symbol of the truth. Unless it be refined and expressed in the passive sexuality practised in Tantric Buddhism and formerly by the troubadours, and also by Betty in her Roman incarnation, it cannot achieve the freedom from time and space produced by the subtler and passionless manifestations of truth I have just mentioned.

To understand these matters more fully we must envisage an ascending scale of people beginning with those individuals whose only moments of self forgetfulness are induced by the brief erupton of sexual intercourse. At the other end of the scale we find highly developed psychics for whom the momentary contact of fingers produces an obliteration of any sense of their apartness as separate personalities and, with it, the timeless experience.

Even with those least dependent on bodily contact there are zones of the body more sensitive than others. Under ordinary circumstances and for ordinary purposes the

172

mucous membrane is more sensitive than the skin. This is why the kiss on the lips can be not only completely passionless but also a transfiguring experience. This is why it was used by the Cathars at the Consolamentum. It is reasonable to assume that contact at what are called the erogenous zones, that is to say those areas of mucous membrane capable of providing, in the average individual, the most intense erotic sensation, have also a greater potential in inducing the timeless experience. This is offset by the fact that the stimulation of the passions is the greatest impediment to self abandonment and for most people the activation of the erogenous zones involves at least the awakening of the erotic sensations. It was all a question of the purpose inspiring these forms of contact. Certainly the flesh itself had been used to attain the level of the spirit. It should be always remembered that the kind of touch which produces self abandonment is always seeking to nullify its own activity to reduce the need for its operation. There comes a stage when, between those on the same wavelength and who have shared the same incarnations, touch, as the instigator of psychic fusion and the timeless experience, can give way to mere presence so that it is only necessary for two people to be together in order to function on a telepathic level and also to see into the past and possibly the future. But this is only given to a few. Graham mentioned it especially because he himself had been capable of it in this life.

He emphasized however the curative possibilities of touch. To bestow peace on another by a touch of the hand or to calm the agitation of a frightened animal is of therapeutic significance. Whenever we are confronted with the elemental situations of life our natural instinct is to touch. When a child is terrified the first impulse of any sensible person is to throw his arms round it. This is basically an attempt to cast out fear by love, to expel the apartness induced by terror by a total harmony conveyed by touch. All the refinements of tactile sensation, even etheric and astral touch, are developments of these primordial and instinctive gestures. No other sense can be used to the same degree in the treatment of disease. Music and art are employed nowadays in therapy. They were used with still

173

greater skill millenia ago. Useful as they are their range of action is never as wide as touch.

Touch is, then, the conductor in the orchestra of sensation. As such it has the power to produce diverse harmonies. Colour, smell, taste and even music can arise from it. It may seem strange that the Cathar revenants should be so concerned with the importance of sensation, all the more seeing that, having died, they have transcended the world of the senses. Dualists have been for so long regarded by their detractors as dour and repressed heretics, and by some of their supporters as impossibly unworldly. Graham made it clear that we are intended to exploit to the full our sensory as distinct from our sensual capacities. Speaking of the Buddhist advice that we close the door on the senses he said that we had mistaken their meaning due to our Western obsessional tendency to distort by over definition. Certainly we can only suffer from the starvation of our senses. Graham advised against enforced ascetecism. There was a world of difference between the repressive discipline of appetites and the realisation that we have outlived the desires and needs of the flesh. Guilhabert de Castres added that sensation is one of the primary aspects of divinity and that Catharism is something to be approached after having comprehended the workings of nature in all its beauty and horror and after having saturated oneself in all the possibilities and potentialities of art. All the sensations must be experienced in their full capacity otherwise they will never consume themselves in the higher function of inner perception. The individual who has never seen a primrose as it truly is should not raise his eyes to God. If he does so a cloud will cross the sun and intensify his myopia. Guilhabert said that it was because they favoured the healthy exploitation of the senses that the Cathars recruited their priesthood so often from those who had lived ordinary married lives and who had separated later by mutual consent. This was unheard of elsewhere in the thirteenth century. The Cathars were not interested in recruiting from over intellectualised youth, over addicted to theology and with perception blunted by a diet of ideas.

The revenants said that the intense and varied sensations

and experiences induced by touch, and especially in its etheric and astral formations, are, in essence, only stepping stones leading to a state of inner perception in which the activity of the senses is no longer necessary. He reminded me that without seeing Betty in this life and before I had seen her in her astral form, I could describe in detail her appearance in her Celtic incarnation. This is the same process as that which enables a minority of those blind from birth to describe in detail people and objects they have never seen. It was very important to realise that the aim of sensation was to dispense with the need for sensation. This could only be achieved by the full exercise of our sensory capacities possibly not in one life but over four or five incarnations.

CHAPTER TWENTY-ONE

Further Revelations: The Sun and the Moon
Mechanisms of Evil. Alchemy

In the preceding chapters I have dealt with a number of the main themes discussed by the revenants. There are other important subjects which I would like to deal with but will refrain from so doing because my understanding of them is imperfect.

Apart from these major topics there were also subjects of immense importance which I only call side issues because of the relatively little time the revenants devoted to them. They added much, for instance, to my knowledge of the nature and the effects of evil. I had always assumed that, in seeking convictions for heresy, the Inquisitors had broken down the accused by the intensity and duration of their interrogations and by physical torture when the victims were handed over to the secular arm. It would be foolish to under-emphasise the influence of such rigorous measures but the revenants told me that these were not the sole mechanisms by which the admission of guilt was extracted from the accused. The Inquisitors had also the capacity to inject the prisoner with a toxic dose of guilt so that he admitted his culpability often without recourse to physical torture. They reminded me that I had myself written, in my book *Obsession** and elsewhere, that one of the principal effects of the power of evil was to induce in the victim an obsessional state based on a suddenly hypertrophied sense of guilt, in which he was prepared to accuse himself of anything. Politely, without undue pressure, there were certain Inquisitors possessed of this power. Some were transmitters of the generalised force of evil, others were possessed. These particular mechanisms operated especially in those cases where the accused admitted himself to be guilty on the first day or early in the proceedings and

* Neville Spearman, 1972.

retracted his admission some days later, after he had recovered a little his moral balance following his separation from the Inquisitors.

There was evidence that in the Middle Ages certain Inquisitors were especially chosen for this purpose. This was a particularly graphic example of the doctrine that the end justifies the means. The fathers of the Church at that time had a greater knowledge of human psychology than we imagine.

The same mechanisms operate to this day. They are well exemplified in the Russian state trials, perhaps less so now than a few years ago. These trials were characterised by the speed and willingness with which the victims inculpated themselves. Once again it was, said the revenants, foolish to minimise the effect of constant interrogations and nights without sleep but the effect of such treatment was not merely to break down the resistance of the victim in the general sense of the term but to render him more vulnerable to the force of evil or to the influence of interrogators possessed by lower entities. The Russians were less aware than the Inquisitors of the mechanisms operating within them. The power of evil they utilised was more calculated to induce guilt than that used by the Gestapo. The latter were more prone to uncomplicated bestiality but this was not to say that Naziism as a whole was not an aspect of diabolism.

Graham discussed a further aspect of the power of evil. He said that this could cause a sudden increase in sexuality. The latter, when stimulated in this way, was not to be regarded as in any sense perverted or evil. He recalled that he himself, in the company of a person he loved but for whom he had no sexual feelings, had felt an unprecedented pang of desire in the company of a monk at a famous Abbey. This unusual feeling was accompanied by appalling terror. His tension and horror were not assuaged until he had run outside and vomited. The stimulation of the sex instinct between couples who had not known it before, or in whom it had died away, was one of nature's methods of protecting them against the force of evil and providing them with the comfort and safeguard of a transient form of unity.

177

Another important subject discussed was the actual nature of the revenants. What was meant by materialisation? It seemed so contradictory to talk of discarnate entities and then to refer to them as materialising. Nevertheless this is what they did, to some extent. In their astral form they were, like us, composed of matter, but in their case its atoms were infinitely small and moving at a different rate of vibration than our own. The revenants said that they themselves were essentially invisible and without form. They acquired the latter and rendered themselves visible to us by their capacity to 'solidify' to some degree the atmosphere around them. They could alter the rhythm of vibrations in their vicinity in such a way that, temporarily, the vibrations of which they were essentially composed were transformed into what were visible to a minority of living beings. The latter were people existing on a special wave-length which enabled them to perceive the vibrations of the air-solidifying revenants. (The latter relatively crude term is used to simplify this issue for me.)

Braïda spoke of this particular subject a good deal before her daughter departed for Canada. The latter had been visited constantly by Braïda, who in the twentieth century was her mother and had died three years previously. The daughter was worried as to whether her deceased mother, who visited her so constantly in England, would continue to do so when she went to Canada. At this time Braïda spoke often of 'changing the system of vibrations' and that it was necessary for a revenant to do so in order to voyage through space. The point she was making, and which I did not see at the time, was that she could so change the system of vibrations as to enable her to cover three thousand miles in an indefinable instant and, at the same time, to retain her capacity to materialise to the degree of rendering herself visible to her daughter in Canada.

These statements of Braïda are of vital importance. They indicate that the capacity of the revenants to appear to us is primarily due to the attributes and gifts of the revenants themselves. The modern rationalist, as well as many people with open minds on these subjects, have long pondered as to whether the revenants we see are outward projections of some process

178

occurring in our minds. Braïda answers this very positively in the negative. The fact that the revenants can only be seen by a minority does not indicate that the latter are projecting, in illusional or hallucinatory form, something out of the recesses of their own unconscious. They are enabled to have these experiences because, while still living, they share to some extent the same vibrational system as the revenants and are thus able to see their materialisation.

*   *   *

Another subject dealt with was the function of the moon in relation to good and evil. The idea that the sun represented good and the moon evil was untenable. It was night and not the moon that was the symbol of evil. While the moon was waxing it had a healing influence. This was revealed in the vegetable and animal kingdoms. It was sound horticulture to plant certain seeds at the waxing of the moon. Similarly at this time the moon reinforced some of those with the gift of healing. Those in whom this gift was accentuated at this time were usually women at whose birth the influence of the moon had been maximal.

The power of the full moon was altogether another matter. It had an adverse effect on some epileptics and schizophrenics. It could increase the incidence of fits in the former and violence in the latter. It had also a harmful effect on the type of obsessional patient riddled with compulsive acts. The latter became worse over the period of the full moon and their sleep was disturbed by nightmares often to be interpreted in terms of mythology.

Where people have a high degree of psychic sensitivity the influence of a full moon can be dramatic because of its power to arouse and augment the energies of the darker entities which surround us. There were two people who in this life achieved a degree of telepathic communication which enabled them to converse without uttering a word and without touching each other. While together on a night with a magnificent full moon the woman became suddenly giddy and fell heavily and the man reeled and was almost knocked down by the attack of a lower entity.

179

For years I entertained the idea that the sun was essentially masculine and the moon feminine. I had been inclined to exaggerate the influence of the latter in the sphere of healing. Now the revenants told me that the sun in its beneficence, warmth and fecundity was inevitably feminine. One could not associate femininity with anything so cold, so distant and, in relation to the sun, so lacking in friendly emanations as the moon. Had I never heard of the man in the moon? The latter folkloric concept was part of a much older wisdom than that which described the sun as male and spoke of the Sun God. The cult of the Sun God was, in fact, a retrograde step from the idea that the sun was feminine. The idea of a Sun King arising in the heavens and having also dominion on earth, was a form of decadence. At one time this idea was basic to Zoroastrianism in Persia. The cult of Mithras at first inherited this idea but as it evolved it rejected the concept of a young hero triumphing on earth and at the same time evolving spiritually in his battle for light against darkness.

The revenants said that this idea of a masculine sun god died hard and had persisted for some time in Mithraic Dualism. They pointed out, however, that in the last two centuries in Rome before its disappearance from the scene, the cult was not exclusive to men. Each sex had faithful and enthusiastic devotees. Their meetings were separate except at certain dates in the year when six representatives from each sect met in a communal gathering. The figure of Mithras with the light radiating from his head was still preserved in the cult but in its last decades Mithras was not worshipped as a deity with strongly masculine attributes. Certainly the cult was strong in the army but its strength there has been exaggerated because the temples of Mithras have so often been discovered near military sites. Far more adherents of this cult worshipped in rooms adapted for the purpose in their own houses which have long since disappeared. In its last years the cult of Mithras owed as much to a European Dualist cult which preceded it as it did to its Middle Eastern sources. A good deal of Mithraic practice at this time derived from the Druids.

The revenants said also that in the last years of Mithraism

there were no animal sacrifices. The slaughter of the Mithraic bull was an allegory symbolising the destruction of the aggressive ego within each of us. All that persisted of animal sacrifice in the fourth century A.D. was the occasional killing of a cock, because the fact that the animal continued to walk after its head had been severed symbolised for the adherents the psyche's independence of the personality.

*　　*　　*

One of the most significant communications made by the discarnates concerned alchemy. I had understood for years that the so-called transmutation of base metal into gold was a symbolic reference to the refinement of our animal nature. I had always found this allegorical explanation unsatisfying. It had the merit of being simple, I had no doubt whatever that it was true for the spiritual transformation we undergo on certain planes of consciousness, but the whole thing remained for me unconvincing. Alchemy had attracted some of the most cultivated and powerful minds in Europe. Surely it embraced something more specific than a rather obvious allegory which could serve as an alphabet for several esoteric systems.

I was fascinated to learn from Guilhabert de Castres one of the deep and highly specific truths of alchemy. He said that the commonest example of true alchemy was unrelated to the transmutation of metals. It was concerned with the transformation of light and with our capacity to see those discarnate entities which still remained in contact with us here on earth. Some of these latter appeared to us in colours, in the features and clothes they had displayed in one or other of their lives on earth. Others appeared outlined in silver. When the outline was perceived to pulsate this was evidence of a higher development in the evolution of the seer. The latter, if he continued to progress, acquired the capacity to see what can be called Christ figures and which used to be known as angels. The latter were revealed in gold and often against a background of golden light. There were still higher experiences in which no form whatever was visible and the individual undergoing the vision was confronted

181

with an indescribable and totally unique light.

Those capable of perceiving such phenomena had attained the level of spiritual experience. The real alchemy, said Guilhabert, lay in the individual's capacity to transform, by increasing insight, the silver of psychic experience, as displayed in seeing the silver outline of such revenants as remain in contact with us on this earth, into the gold of spiritual experience in which we can see the gold of the Christ figures and of the vibrating centres of healing and goodness which lie beyond them.

*　　*　　*

These direct communications from the revenants are necessary because they represent revealed truth in its full cosmic significance. At this stage in world history it is more than ever necessary to realise that there are people able to function out of time and to see the past and the future. It is from such people that the prophets of the world have been and are still recruited. It may be that there is still a majority which does not accept that Paul was enlightened by a vision on the road to Damascus, that Mohammed had a similar experience and that Christ had access to sources of truth denied to us. Be this as it may I myself can say that, without aspiring to be a prophet, I have been in touch with several wise men and women now dead who have seen into the mysteries of life and nature and who bring us truth from the higher strata of consciousness which follow death. It should also be born in mind that I have done this before,* recording what I was told seven hundred years ago by Guilhabert de Castres in a manuscript which was essentially an expanded and simplified commentary on a smaller work which he himself had written. I am only repeating in the idom of my age what I did before and which was lost in the course of years.

What I have written in these chapters devoted to personal communications reveals not only more of the nature of Catharism but of its sources. The preoccupation with the creation of the world, and the emanatory theories associated with it, are markedly Gnostic. There is more I could have written but I

* See *The Lake And The Castle*, Neville Spearman, London.

have produced enough to show that Catharism was not an obscure and ephemeral heresy but a comprehensive scientific and philosophic concept of the nature of the universe.

INDEX

People and places about which the author gives information have been indexed but passing mentions have not been included.

185